DOSTOEVSKY

DOSTOEVSKY

by EDUARD THURNEYSEN

Translated by Keith R. Crim

WIPF & STOCK · Eugene, Oregon

A translation of *Dostojewski* by Eduard Thurneysen, originally
published by Zwingli Verlag, Zürich/Stuttgart, 1963.

Wipf and Stock Publishers
199 W 8th Ave, Suite 3
Eugene, OR 97401

Dostoevsky
By Thurneysen, Eduard and Crim, Keith
Copyright©1964 by Thurneysen, Eduard
ISBN 13: 978-1-60899-581-3
Publication date 6/10/2010
Previously published by John Knox Press, 1964

CONTENTS

If the experiment has made any impression at all, then it must be as when the beating of the wings of a wildfowl is heard above the heads of the tame fowl of the same species, who live secure in the sureness of reality, and brings them involuntarily to beat their wings, because each beat of the wings is at the same time anxiety—and allurement.

KIERKEGAARD

I | What Is Man?

Whoever comes to Dostoevsky from the regions of secure humanity, of the pre-war period for instance, must feel like one who has been looking at such domesticated animals as the dog and the cat, the chicken or the horse, and then suddenly sees the Wild before him, and without warning finds himself face to face with the yet untamed animal world, jaguar and puma, tiger and crocodile, the slithering of the snakes and the fluttering of the wings of the eagle and the condor. He is surrounded by awesome wildness, by strangeness, by the riddle of nature that has not yet been conquered, not yet contained and controlled, not yet crippled and chained by a hundred safety devices. "He has entered primeval territory" (Stefan Zweig). Far beyond him lie all inhabited, comfortable, and mild regions. He has been led out past the farthermost border posts, past the limits of known humanity; with pounding heart he looks on the unknown face of a man who shares with him the common name of "man," and who yet appears to live beyond all the concepts tied with this name, beyond good and evil, wisdom and folly, beauty and ugliness, beyond even state and family, school and church. And just as the one who returns from the wilderness to domesticated animals rediscovers in the four-footed creatures who share his house, and whom he had previously regarded sympathetically, the traces of original wildness, and sees himself even in his own four walls confronted at a stroke with dangerous, unsuspected slumbering possibilities, so there proceeds from an encounter with the world and the men of Dostoevsky something of hidden trembling and fear. "The glance into chaos" has its consequences, and Hermann Hesse's[1] call, as that of a sentinel filled with hidden concern, in which he has so urgently pointed out the connection between the Russian men and women of Dostoevsky and the decline of the West, was not raised without good reason. The uncanny outbursts of an inscrutable humanity, such as Dostoevsky reveals to us, have something deeply stirring and disquieting in them. Without difficulty they bring sleepless hours at night and eerie dreams by day to the one who draws near to them. Latzko's characters in *Men in War*,* thanks to their gruesomely exaggerated situation, must have made an especially frightening impression on weak-nerved neutrals; Dostoevsky's men live in the profound peace of Russian cities of the sixties and seventies of the last century; no grenades are bursting, no mounds of corpses are heaped up, no barbed wire looms. Everything takes place in the midst of a gray, trivial, everyday existence. But this only makes the faces of an incredibly different, dark nature of man, hidden behind and under the veil of this gray, everyday life, all the more threatening, all the truer. Could it not be that beneath the surface of our seemingly so well-ordered life also there slumbers the fiery glow of a primordial life full of problems not coped with and mystery not explained—or perhaps it is no longer slumbering?

We all know the characteristic dizziness that seizes us when we come too close to a train that is traveling in the same direction as we are. We lose at once the sure path on

[1] Hermann Hesse, *Blick ins Chaos*, Bern, 1920.

* Trans. note: English edition of this novel published by Boni and Liveright, New York, 1918.

which we were going; we stumble; we are even in actual danger of falling under the wheels that roll past us. An encounter with Dostoevsky's men and women has an effect not much different. They stride past us in visionary strangeness and size and yet in strange proximity, in the same direction, almost like our doubles, so that involuntarily we stumble and cannot continue on our way with the same certainty. We would like to disclaim anything in common with these figures, and yet we are unable to do so. For in the riddle of *their* lives we are confronted in an undeniably moving manner with the riddle of our *own* lives. Caught by this we could like to say, "Whom have we met?" And yet we know, before we ask, that we have met ourselves, that we have met *mankind.* But what does that mean, "To meet mankind"? What is this "we ourselves"? What is "mankind"?

This is Dostoevsky's question and ours. Because we cannot avoid this question, today less than ever, we can therefore not avoid the encounter with Dostoevsky. For it is the destiny—and the supreme mastery—of Feodor Mikhailovich Dostoevsky that he was constrained by this question to an unprecedented degree and that he phrased it in such comprehensive breadth and compelling depth that in his works all related questions stream together as in a gigantic catchment basin. That gives his existence as man that almost legendary greatness, uniqueness, and necessity. Stefan Zweig has expressed it marvelously in his study on Dostoevsky.[2] But that also unwittingly makes his work the great critical dividing point which all significant thought systems of the close of the nineteenth century must encounter, and which determines their failure or success. For that which moves, disquiets, and chills the spirits and sensibilities, the brains and nerves of the men of this time with need and hope, with passion, torment,

---

[2] Stefan Zweig, *Drei Meister,* Inselverlag, 1920.

and longing, with intuitions of coming terror and distant
paths of redemption, all that also loomed around Dostoevsky,
led him through its experiences, moved him, tormented him.
Nothing human remained foreign to him. He foresaw and
anticipated Zarathustra-Nietzsche's discovery and message of
the decline of man, and also his titanic lunge toward the
Superman. He himself led Ibsen's attack on society, but ten
times stronger than Ibsen did. Without knowing Kierkegaard
or Overbeck, he bore in himself the deepest mistrust toward
a Christendom that had become church, and he loved in his
Russian church just that which is *not* church in it—the re-
minders, still preserved pure, as he believed, of the early history of Christendom, free from compromise. He did not stand
aloof from the contest for a final reconciliation of culture and
conscience, such as filled the discordant soul of his con-
temporary Tolstoy, but lent it powerful expression himself.
Above all he recognized clearly the total undermining of the
bases of the economy, the moth-eaten nature of social morality
in all European lands, and he heard from the depths the cry
of enslaved mankind. He saw the greatness of the wrath that
was stored up everywhere against a day of wrath. He also
saw the approach of this day himself and proclaimed ahead of
time all his fearfulness in prophetic words. For he knew the
power of released demons as only few did; he knew to what
the revolt of man breaking out of his prisons in a blind rage
must lead. And so he unites in himself the whole many-sided
striving of the European soul at the end of the nineteenth
century and holds the mirror up to it. Whoever looks into it
reads something of the nameless disquiet, the deep skepti-
cism, the torment and defiance, and the unallayed longing of
this unfortunate epoch, which was being driven into the abyss
of war and revolution. Dostoevsky wrote its legends while it
was still around him on every side. It is not without cause that
one has the feeling that those spokesmen of the epoch who

embody most powerfully the riddle of the time—I would mention especially Nietzsche and Tolstoy, and could add Lenin to them—are figures out of the works of Dostoevsky. To this extent he saw everything, knew about everything, and drew into the spell of his work everything that inwardly motivated the entire era!

For all that, he was not a historian; no, not at all. He certainly undertook no "studies"—as they are called—of the nineteenth century. He was scarcely acquainted to any extent with material in foreign languages. He traveled much, but with eyes strangely directed inward, and outwardly closed like those of a sleepwalker. Abroad he read many newspapers, but almost exclusively Russian ones. One thing remains. He had an incomparable sensitivity for everything that was in the air. And he himself possessed in the highest degree what he boasted of, in his speech on Pushkin, as the Russian characteristic par excellence, the ability to enter completely into foreign spirits. Still all that does not explain his magical power that could master all human affairs, even the most hidden. His secret does not lie in being able to guess all sorts of secrets, nor in the knowledge of all sorts of hidden matters. His secret lies in the fact that he knew that we still know nothing even when we know many things. It does not lie in personal presuppositions of a psychic nature, which others may possess in common with him without being what he was. On the contrary, it lies in what Karl Nötzel[3] has called his complete *lack* of presuppositions. His secret is really nothing but that question, his question about man. It lies in the fact that he carried nothing in himself except the one great, endless penetrating concern to get to the basis of all things. "I *inquire* constantly about everything," says Prince Myshkin, his favorite character in *The Idiot*, as if he would make

---

[3] Karl Nötzel, *Dostoevsky und Wir*, Munich, 1920.

Dostoevsky's own secret known. But because all things on earth, as soon as one questions them as to where they come from and where they are going, point back like beams of light to man as the point from which they receive their value or lack of value, their light or shadow, man becomes the great riddle on which are fixed the deeply penetrating eyes of this questioner who has no presuppositions. But even in relation to man he does not stop at anything creaturely, given, penultimate, even if it were the finest psychic depth conceivable. It is in relation to man that the entire power of his freedom from presuppositions is first awakened and exerts itself. "It all depends on the discovery of life, the uninterrupted, the eternal discovery, and not at all on what is discovered," reads another passage in *The Idiot*. This Socratic wisdom is Dostoevsky's wisdom and the total, the ultimate, secret of his art. Because man has become a riddle for him, therefore and therein he has understood man so deeply.

Once again, What is man? Dostoevsky raised this question; more he did not do. It could seem to be little, and yet it is immeasurably great, for in him it becomes clear that this question, truly asked, is not only question, but is itself already the answer. With relentless severity Dostoevsky drives the tunnels of his analysis in the mines of his formulations one after the other until the most secret depths are reached, the utmost bounds. Even the most extreme results of psychoanalytic research have already been anticipated in his work. The whole naïve immediacy of human existence, with all the splendor and enchantment that can lie upon it, whether it be moralistic, or aesthetic, or religious in nature, collapses into itself, stripped bare by his hands. The end of man is the end of all the roads on which Dostoevsky accompanies him. And yet the works of Dostoevsky shine as if illumined from within with the secret, no longer earthly light of a powerful, an ultimate synthesis. Not decline, not contemptuous laughter over men of whom the devil has made fools, but the incomprehensible word of victory, "resurrection," is the last word of his novels.

"They wanted to speak, but could not. Tears stood in their eyes. They were both pale and gaunt, but in these sick and pale faces the dawn of a new future was shining, of a full resurrection to new life." These are the final sentences of *Crime and Punishment*.

And out of Mitya Karamazov's prison at the end of *The Brothers Karamazov* come the words, "Alyosha, in these two months I have discovered a new man in myself; a new man has been resurrected in me! This man was always hidden within me, but I would have never become conscious of having him within me if God had not sent the storm. This life is strange! But what does it matter that I will work with a sledgehammer in Siberian mines for twenty years. That does not frighten me anymore. I am afraid of something entirely different, and that is my only great anxiety. I am afraid that the man who has been resurrected in me may leave me again."

It is from those darkest depths into which his analysis has penetrated that the wonderful light of this new synthesis streams forth. From prisons, yes, only from prisons, do such words as those of Mitya Karamazov arise, and this dawn of a new future lies only on "pale and gaunt faces." "Only where there are graves is there resurrection" (Nietzsche). That is neither coincidence nor a refined technique of contrast used by writers. A deeper purpose is there. Here we do not have mere pragmatism, but recognition. These visible contrasts hint at invisible connections. These apparently disconnected transitions in the foreground witness to significant developments in the hidden background. The fearful crisis which Dostoevsky sees breaking over the whole human world is full of a turning toward salvation. From death to life; that is what it means. The nearness and common source of this recognition, not only with Socratic wisdom—we have already referred to that—but also with biblical insight, is unmistakable. That must be said above all if something true is to be said about Dostoevsky. For only here is his whole greatness, the whole breadth of the connections in which he stands, revealed. It is this that gives his work that absolutely conclusive character, that character so superior to Ibsen, Strindberg, Jacobsen, who are in their own way also analysts of the first rank. It is this that gives his novels their classic maturity despite their monstrous lack of form. It is for this that we love them, not for the radical nature of their negations, but for their still greater affirmations, which arise from their denials.

But that is it; they arise from the *denials.* Like the Anthony of the Isenheim altar piece, who can see God's face on high only in the midst of the hell of demonic assault, so the dawn of the new day which is visible in Dostoevsky's work breaks forth only in the deepest night of human uncertainty. Dostoevsky's own words are witness of this. "My Hosanna has passed through the great purging fire of doubt." Therefore it remains thus. Dostoevsky does not have any final answer or solution to give to us. His solution is found in the great dissolution; his answer is a question, the one burning question of the being of man. But anyone who takes up this question will experience that even this question is full of answers.

II | Dostoevsky's Men and Women

A group of remarkable people, people from all classes of society and all imaginable and possible spiritual provinces and zones between heaven and hell, have all been seized from out of the midst of life and placed into life like the peasant figures of Jeremias Gotthelf. Thus they are no spooks and shadows, but real people of reality, with earthly names and faces, having grown, in all phases of their being, one with the ground on which they stand, and yet all just in their earthly nature so strangely unearthly, just in their reality so completely not of this world, just in their belonging so uprooted! Their life is banal and trivial, just as life is. We have only to think of the locale of most of Dostoevsky's novels—dark alleys, narrow rooms, dubious taverns, brothels, and prisons; but in just these dark corners what ecstasies of the soul soaring to all the heavens, what plunges into all depths take place! The bare walls of these narrow cells and rooms echo with what unheard-of conversations, and these brick walls of poverty-stricken suburbs are surrounded by what thoughts and dreams; the triviality and banality of *this* life is latent with the secret of a wholly *other* life! That is Dostoevsky's world, those are his men and women, that is his answer so full of questions, his question full of knowledge!

But let us step closer.

Rodion Raskolnikoff. A young student living in poverty and humble circumstances. His strong, proud spirit is depressed by the narrowness of his existence. In his miserable room it seems to him that he is shut up in a coffin. He seeks a way out. Why should he not simply break out of his confines, carry his will through, with force if necessary, or even over top of a corpse? He knows a usurious old woman. What is her life worth in comparison with his? What if he killed her and took her possessions?—Is this not a realistic and decisive thought? That is the way Napoleon thought, if he thought at all; at least it is the way he acted. "A true ruler, to whom everything is permissible, destroys Toulon, arranges a massacre in Paris, forgets an army in Egypt, uses up half a million men in a Russian campaign, and in Vilna dismisses the affair with a pun. And after his death statues are erected to him; so therefore everything is permissible. No, such people are obviously not made out of flesh and blood, but out of iron!" What prevents the student from also thinking this way, from also acting this way? "Extraordinary men," he thinks, "have the right to step over certain hindrances when the fulfillment of their ideas demands it." Still, something hinders him. To be sure, he is "an extraordinary man," and he has "an idea," or rather it has him, but it is obviously not so simple to step over all hindrances. It is obviously not so simple to be made of iron instead of flesh and blood. Oh, this mysterious something that he cannot get past! Is it outside him? Is it within him? Are there aesthetic scruples that hold him back from murder? Are there moral prejudices, "the Schiller in him that becomes rebellious every moment," as Svidrigailoff taunts? Enough, it is there! But with casuistry sharp as a knife it is attacked. Certainly it is only a spook. It must be throttled. For the strong, no scruples and prejudices are valid. "Everything is permissible." The way is free, and as a sign of

this the murder ax falls. A victory is won. Or, is it in the end
not won? In the moment when the ax descended was it not
already infinitely clear that the something had *not* been overcome? Else why did the murderer carry out his deed so much
against his nature, so lamely, so inhibitedly, "as if," says
Dostoevsky, "someone had taken him by the hand and led
him along irresistibly and unresisting . . . as if he himself
were being led to execution . . . as if the corner of his coat had
been caught in the wheel of a machine and he were being
carried along with it?" And after the deed, how strangely
uprooted and lost the strong one seems! He hides the stolen
goods not only from the police but also from himself. He is in
flight without being pursued. And his rising above all scruples
ends by his going and turning himself in. Instead of setting
himself up victoriously like a god, he lets himself be humiliated by Sonia the harlot, bows to the earth, and kisses it like
a penitent, and is banished to Siberia. And now he stands
squarely before the inexpressible something of life itself,
which had tortured and persecuted him, and which he yet,
with all his sharp-edged dialectic, had not been able to discover, and with his deed had not been able to clasp to himself.

The inexpressible something of life itself—yes, that is
what it was which, not understood by him, had stood in the
midpoint of all Raskolnikoff's dreams and speculations from
his childhood on. "Where was it that I read," he says once to
himself, "how one sentenced to death speaks or thinks one
hour before his death, that if he were permitted to live somewhere on a height, on a cliff, and on a narrow strip where he
could merely place his two feet—surrounded by abysses, by
the ocean, by eternal darkness, eternal loneliness and eternal
storm,—and so, standing on this yard-wide strip, had to pass
his whole life, a thousand years, an eternity,—that it would
be better to live like that than to die at once! Only live, live,

live! How? No matter! Just live! . . . How true! Lord God, how true!" In such words full of insatiable thirst for life, the hidden mainspring and presupposition of all his thoughts lies revealed. This intellectual and theoretician thirsts for *life*, not for murder and death. "If I had somehow continued on my way, I would never have committed another murder," he says later when he has learned to understand himself. He seeks in all his casuistry that which is more than all casuistry. Therefore he sharpens it "like a razor." Therefore he pushes it to the utmost point, to the point where it—so he thinks— comprehends the final contradictions and must unconditionally be turned into the sought-for, fully positive, and immediate nature of life itself, into the royal possession of which he seeks to enter.

In Raskolnikoff the question concerning life is asked with all the weight which the commitment of the total man can give it; not only something about life, not a little piece of life, but life, life itself, life in the full creative sense of the word is demanded. But such a demand no longer lies within the area of human possibilities. If it did, it would then be not merely the area of *human* possibilities. Life is in *God*. In him are its sources. He is the creator. Man, however, is not God. Or is he? Raskolnikoff faces this audacious question. That is the core of his problem. He is concerned with this Promethean encroachment. "I did not kill in order to help my mother— that is nonsense! I did not kill in order to gain means and power and then become a benefactor of mankind. Nonsense! I killed simply for myself. It was for myself alone that I killed. Whether I should have become someone's benefactor, or whether I would have spent my whole life like a spider catching all in my web,—that must have been to me in that moment a matter of total indifference! . . . I was not primarily concerned with money when I killed; it was not money that was so important to me, but something entirely different. . . .

Now I know it all. . . . I had to experience something else; something else drove me to it. Then it was I had to find out as quickly as possible whether I am a louse like the rest, or a man! Am I able to rise above them or not? Will I dare to bend down and grasp power or not? Am I a trembling creature or not?" Here he is interrupted by Sonia. But we know enough. Nietzsche's *Ecce homo* is near. The boundaries of humanity are to be displaced. Here it is a matter of the purity of the concepts: God, man, and life!

And the solution? We have hinted at it. When he had pushed his dialectic to the uttermost point, there where the boundaries between heaven and earth, between God and man disappear, where man grasps for the life of God, it breaks, not in life, but in death. The deed which this Promethean logic produces is the non-deed, murder. But it is exactly here that comprehension is found. It now becomes infinitely clear that man is *not* God. Even the "strong one" is "a miserable louse like all the rest." It is not within the realm of human power to lay hold of life in creative immediacy. No theory, not even the most refined, can open the access here. It can be grasped in no deed. In the recognition of this fact Raskolnikoff awakens. "In what way, in what way," he thought, "is my idea more stupid than the other ideas and theories which whirl around and bounce off each other in the world as long as it exists? You need only to consider the matter from a fully independent standpoint, distant and freed from everyday influences, and then certainly my thought does not appear so strange. . . . He faced the torment of this question and . . . surmised the deep lie in his convictions." Only now does he understand himself. Only now does he understand God. And only now does he understand himself in God and from God precisely in his finiteness and humanity. He no longer strives to overcome it, for he knows that from *man's* side there is no bridge that leads across; there is none for the sake of God's honor and man's purity. But, perhaps from *God's* side? That is no longer a Promethean question, for it is no longer a question of human possibilities. In this question Raskolnikoff opens for himself the view of a final possibility of really passing over into the eternal kingdom of life, the possibility of resurrection. But this final possibility of man is no longer a possibility of *man*. Yet whoever has passed like Raskolnikoff into the knowledge and fear of God must know of just this final and unique, this impossible possibility, and will be able to know of it without danger. Once already it had appeared before him when Sonia, the harlot, had read to the murderer in that incomprehensible night, full of confession and humiliation, the story of the raising of Lazarus (this story of resurrection!) from the Gospel of John. He did not understand it then, but now that inconceivably great word is even on *his* lips, that word that says more than man can know, the word "resurrection."

"A new outlook on life" is what Dostoevsky in one place calls the result of the total upheaval that took place in Raskolnikoff. Well, just one more theory? Once more only an idea, a thought? That is what we might be tempted to ask. Yes, just another theory, just one more thought is the result of this struggle. But a *new* thought, a *new* theory, "a *new* outlook on life." We have heard what it consists of, of the recognition that the true, the proper life of man lies beyond man as he is here and now, beyond the highest boundary of what we customarily call life. However, this is not for the purpose of showing again a way of laying hold on this true life and triumphantly taking advantage of it, not in order to win from the tragedy of a so-called intellectual the password, "life is more than theory and thought," and then with this password to discredit thought altogether and rule it out in favor of a more than questionable "experience." Truly, *Crime and Punishment* was not written for that purpose. Precisely not for that! But certainly only in order to lead *thought* about life in the right paths, and to distinguish a false thought from the true. If that seems too little, let the reader attempt anew, with the romantics and pseudo-revolutionaries of all shades, whether he might not succeed, surpassing Raskolnikoff, through the most radical turns and breakthroughs to force his access to a superhuman life beyond all limits that bind us here and now. He will only relive in his own way the tragedy of Raskolnikoff. His "new outlook on life" was not too little for Dostoevsky. It was not too little for him that at the end of his book there was neither a revolutionary nor a pacifist, neither a particularly pure, noble soul, a martyr or saint nor a dilletante and reformer, not even a fully repentant man to be seen, but "only" a man, who had "a new outlook on life," and who now very simply, while still burdened with all the problems of his character, under the judgment and under the promise of this new outlook again faces life as it is here and now.

On earth that may be little, but in heaven there is more joy over *one* sinner who repents than over ninety-nine just persons who have no need of repentance.

The Brothers Karamazov. A father and three sons, and in their midst a woman for whom they desperately struggle with one another. A servant solves the conflict by murdering the father, and in so doing he believes he is in agreement with Ivan, one of the sons. But another son, Mitya, is suspected of the murder, judged guilty, and sent to Siberia. The youngest, Alyosha, seeks and finds a deeper meaning in this senseless brew of titanic passions that have broken loose. You might call it a fantastic story, incredible in its whole compass. And yet, is there a *truer* story anywhere? It is not in vain that this time there stands, not as in *Crime and Punishment,* an idea, but *woman,* in the focus of their storms and catastrophes.

Woman. What then is woman? Listen to the answer: Her

name is Grushenka. And a few words stammered out of the
fullness of the passion and despair of those she bewitched and
deceived may serve to illuminate her riddle. "A common
harlot, with whom I would not care to be related," says her
relative Rakitin, who pursues her secretly. "A courtesan," the
old Karamazov agrees, and then continues in a strange out-
burst to a pair of monks, "This common creature, this woman
that leads a disreputable life, is perhaps holier than you gentle-
men, you who are seeking the salvation of your souls." "This
woman is an animal." "This girl is an angel; I know how bewitching she is, but also how good she is," are further judgments. But the earthquake that she causes is mirrored most
powerfully in the ecstatic words of Mitya Karamazov. "Yes,
that's what she is, a tiger, the queen of shamelessness, the
wholly infernal woman, the queen of all infernal women that
you can ever imagine in the world."

Strangely the impression that the pure Alyosha has of her
when he sees her for the first time agrees with these conflict-
ing judgments. "The portals were thrown back, and Grushenka stepped smiling into the room. Alyosha felt something
pierce him. His whole glance at once surrounded her, and he
could not turn his eyes away from her. So that was she, this
fearsome woman, the 'animal' as Ivan had expressed himself
about her a half hour before. A strong, full figure with soft,
almost noiseless movements of her body. She did not come
with firm steps; no, she drew near inaudibly. No step could
be heard on the floor. Softly she lowered herself into the
armchair, softly rustled her splendid black silk dress, and
daintily covered her full neck, white as foam, and her broad
shoulders with an expensive black shawl. She was twenty-two
years old, and her face expressed this age exactly. Her com-
plexion was very white, and only her cheeks had a pale red
shimmer. . . . Her magnificent, rich, dark blond hair, the
dark, finely drawn eyebrows, and her wonderful gray-brown

eyes with the long lashes could have forced the most indifferent and distracted man, no matter where, in a crowd, on a stroll, in the press of the streets, suddenly to stop before this face and to keep it long in his memory. Most of all, the naïve, good-natured expression of this face affected Alyosha. She looked at him like a child. . . . Her look rejoiced the heart, Alyosha felt. But there was something else in her which he could not explain to himself, perhaps because he did not understand it, something that communicated itself to him unconsciously, namely this softness, tenderness of her body's movements, this noiselessness of her steps, like those of a cat." That is Grushenka, the woman. And, on the other side, the Karamazovs. "Now these three carnal men observed each other with knives in their boot legs," said Dostoevsky. And yet they are father and sons! That is the exposition of this drama; the wild whirl of the action which develops out of it forms the content of this astonishing book.

Raskolnikoff was bewitched by his idea. But the bewitching of man by the beauty of woman unleashes entirely different hurricanes of passion, calls in a totally different way to incalculable recklessness, to titanic storming of heaven and to demonic plunges to hell. The acme of the enchantment of man is the bewitching through *Eros*. Here man first learns to know all his heights and depths; here he first sees what he is capable of. Burning folly, cold, soulless calculation, boundless pride, the urge to abase others, prodigious, violent self-exaltation, and the wild force of self-contempt, even to the point of self-destruction, wantonness of cruelty and of love. Thus it surges up and down in the changing current. Man becomes godlike and devilish; for if anywhere, it is in the erotic that the parable of divine possibilities and realities is given.

With the parable, however, there is also given the titanic temptation of the *eritis sicut deus* (Ye shall be like God), the temptation to make out of the parable and allusion more than parable and allusion, the seduction to be superman, to be the man-god. In this seductive ambiguity lies the special danger of the zone in which Grushenka reigns, and the Karamazovs are enflamed by it. The beauty of woman seems to break out of all logical and ethical contexts, out of all perceptible continuity with the rest of life. "Beauty is a riddle" is therefore the definition that is given in *The Idiot.* That is to say, it appears before the astonished, easily deceived eye of man as a value which surpasses in its incomprehensibility and underivability all other values, as the epitome of life itself. It is as if there existed what can never exist for us anywhere, as if it would embody what can never become flesh and blood: the immediacy of life, the Olympian springtime, the apotheosis of mankind. For this reason then, the fascination, the madness, the intoxication of man for woman, and of woman for man, so easily exceeds all measure. That is the magic of the erotic. And it is just that, *magic.*

Already in their ascent of Olympus the enchanted ones meet the downward procession of dethroned gods, and if they are wise they will consider that they, too, must die. From the very first, together with the possibility of intoxication and seduction, there is given the superior possibility of resisting the enchantment, of awakening out of the seduction, of sanctifying the limits,—of knowing *God.* There where after titantic usurpations the unavoidable plunge to the depths follows, yes, there the dreamed of, usurped heaven can no longer be confused with the *true* heaven. When the erotic dream in which men and women dream of becoming gods is over, then perhaps there is enough sobriety and prudence at hand to enable one to see the especially strict inviolability of the boundaries here in this area. But where the confusion no longer exists, where—inevitably amid tortures and disappointments—the insight into the especially deep confinement of man as man and of woman as woman begins to become clear, there it is not far to the longing for a new and totally different form of mankind where there will be neither male nor female. And in this yearning there is perception of divine truth, for that is a yearning for something that is not accessible to man's grasping, a yearning for resurrection. At the end of the book, with this longing on their lips, Mitya Karamazov and Grushenka, the infernal woman, stand before the gates of heaven, tired of the Odyssey of their passions.

The strange shy boy Alyosha with his faith, and the starets Zossima, who stands behind him, and from whose mouth originate Alyosha's remarkable insights, all this deep interpretation of all happenings (even the most confused, which is always somehow present in these two figures, if only on the perimeter, or to speak with Wolynski,[4] the white cloister walls on the edge of the Karamazov world), this possibility of accepting life as they both accept it, as those who perceive, know, interpret, this almost uncannily great, heavy possibility can move from the perimeter into the center, can itself become the theme of the tale. This happened in what is perhaps Dostoevsky's most profound creation, *The Idiot.*

The Idiot. Prince Myshkin, an epileptic, returns to Russia from a nerve clinic in Switzerland without being cured. A pleasant, shy man, full of goodness and of the simplicity of a child. "His eyes were large and blue," we read of him, "and when he looked at a person he did not avert his glance. His voice was soft and peaceful." His contacts with people were characterized by strange informality and naïveté, and he seemed destined always to bring up the rear, to appear ridiculous everywhere, to be taken advantage of by all. And that is the way it turned out. From the first scene on, where in the General's waiting room he does not know at all how to behave

---

[4] A. L. Wolynski, *Das Reich der Karamasoff,* Munich, 1920.

toward the servant, to that soiree where, newly engaged, he
pours out his heart in an uninhibited flow of words to a circle
of persons from the highest society, and when he reaches the
climax, with an awkward gesture breaks a costly Chinese vase,
his social faux pas, his painful embarrassments, his lamentably
clumsy acts are without number. What is this man doing in
the world? This question accompanies him inevitably from
the moment of his first appearance. But now the remarkable
thing happens that at once turns this question around so that
instead of being directed by others to him, in ever increasing
measure it is addressed by him to the others. This absolute
fool begins to turn the world upside down; this one who is
poor in spirit gives the clever and wise something to think
about; this defenseless man reveals himself as the only one
who is truly strong, this harmless one as a destroyer. His
clumsiness and fearlessness become a stone of offense on which
the social forms and conventions of the world shatter and are
broken. His ignorance of a thousand objects of human knowledge brings the suspension and devaluation of these things.
His naïveté is irrepressible and causes profound discomfort.
His whole lack of purpose in his contacts with people becomes
the key that opens all doors to him; the absence of any
conceit, any lust for power, forces others to put their confi-
dence in him, to be subject to him. A pair of fearsome persons,
Nastasia, a harlot, and Rogozhin, who is under her spell,
appear near him as if they were the only ones congenial to
him. Appalling developments take place. The Idiot is in love
with the harlot. Yes, but what does "love" mean for him?
The other murders her out of jealousy, and finally the two
men spend a last night beside the corpse of the woman over
whom they had contended, as she lies still and cold between
them, "as if spewed out by the sea of passions" (Wolynski).[5]

---

[5] A. L. Wolynski, *Das Buch vom grossen Zorn*, Frankfort, 1905.

But even in the realm of such unheard-of men and events, even in the realm of the erotic, Prince Myshkin the Idiot appears as the only one not under a spell, the only one who knows, who is above it all, and therefore basically the most uncanny of them all. Yet he remains the child, simpleminded, strange to life, epileptic, and it is just as such that he is all that he is.

Truly, like a single great question it comes from him: Is the meaning of life buried so deep then that the wise man who perceives it can appear among us only as one misunderstood, only as a fool, the strong man who holds it in his hands, only as weak, the healthy man who draws his nourishment from it, only as sick? Is then the true interpretation, the meaning of all that happens on earth, so fully crowded out into the margin that only those who themselves are in some way out there—harlots, murderers, and the insane—can follow its trail and understand it? And that, wherever this meaning, this interpretation, is brought again into the center, it immediately seems to be a disruption of all that is customary—ridiculous naïveté, idiocy, something totally foreign, unprecedentedly different from everything that has previously happened and been thought?

To push the paradox to the limit, how the Idiot draws his deepest insights, "beauty, greatness, eternity, the inspired flowing together with the highest synthesis of life, wherein God is seen," as he expresses it, out of those moments when the dreadful spasm of his sickness seizes him and he collapses, foaming at the mouth! Much has already been said and surmised about the psychology and pathology of this remarkable source of knowledge, and all the more so since Dostoevsky is here only recounting his own experiences. He himself suffered from the mysterious holy sickness, and he ascribed to its outbreaks and spasms the highest value for insight. But it is not the psychological element, neither the heightened sensitivity, nor the mystic ecstasy that is the essential in this enigmatic moment. The essential element in it is, as Myshkin once said, that it is only the "*pre*-monition of that other second when the attack occurs with a dreadful scream, in which at once everything human disappears." The essential element is the similarity of this moment with the last moments of a person who is to be executed, immediately before the ax descends. The essential element is the nearness of the absolute moment of death which it brings with it. And again it is Dostoevsky's own experience, when he speaks of the remarkable light that falls on life from such a moment of death. He experienced it himself as a young man when he was about to be shot on the Semenovsky Regiment's drill field in Petersburg. He never forgot those minutes before the execution. They were "the most intense moment of his life" (Zweig). He learned from death how to understand life. His whole, uniquely deep perception of life could rightly be called "death-wisdom." In any case, when one like Dostoevsky-Myshkin draws his final insight into life from a moment that can be compared only to death, his vision and understanding of everything will necessarily be light-years removed from that everyday vision and understanding from which we are accustomed to gain our knowledge of the world and life. By this we can measure the force of the questioning of this usual knowledge of the world and life which arises here, but we must also measure by it the distinctiveness, meaning, and magnitude of the position heralded by the radical nature of such a negation.

It is almost too audacious to speak here of a "position." (Although it is here above all that we must speak of one.) For the attitude which the Idiot assumes is different, totally different from all attitudes which we receive from teaching desk, from pulpit, and around the family table, and which we are otherwise accustomed to regard as "position," and from that which we are tempted to accept as a positive, as an affirmative, fruitful relation to life, different, totally different from what is commonly called "attitude." To be sure, he is constantly surrounded by persons, who in spite of all resistance feel themselves strangely drawn to him. Strange twists and turns take place around him, as if some magnetic field surrounded him. Unmistakably far-reaching blessings go out from him. Deeply embittered persons become tender as children before him; the proud become humble; completely closed persons open out. Shame and regret are awakened in the depraved; the intense hatred of rivals in love is disarmed; and tears flow from eyes that had not wept for years.

What indicates perhaps more strongly than anything else a hidden positiveness is the fact that children are the Idiot's best friends. The pages of this book are filled with indescribably tender scenes of children. It would, however, be a highly perverse judgment to seek to draw from this a picture of the general friend of adults and children. The Prince completely lacks the necessary traits of friendly humaneness, mild approachability, direct winsomeness, perhaps also of diligent inclination to teach. He is not a so-called "Johannine figure." The main attribute of his nature is its completely cryptic character. That which is affirmative and positive in his attitude is always the totally incomprehensible, because it is invisible and inaccessible, and it always works only indirectly and can be deduced only indirectly. The blessing that emanates from him, the answer which he represents, is incomparable with any other of the manifold answers, the friendliness, the edifying impressions which characterize the usual friend of man. Even this strange saint's friendships with children begin significantly—as elsewhere in Dostoevsky—with their most pronounced rejection of him. He has no intention of being kind to children, of blessing, comforting, influencing, teaching, pouring out himself toward all sides.

Nowhere can anything of that sort be detected in him. "Now I am going out among people," he says once at the beginning of the book. "Perhaps they will not understand me. Perhaps I will have a difficult time among them and feel lonely. But I will be honorable and open to all, and certainly no one would demand more of me than that." That is his program; but it is no program, no visible position, no recognizable goal. And again, what is visible in him is always his *not* being that which others are—that is, his directness, his timidity, modesty, shyness. His tremendous ignorance of how to deal with reality, his not being able to come to terms with it, are again and again the cause of his defeat, are again and again merely the indication that he has nothing to represent that others could grasp.

Illustrative of this is the scene, which Hermann Hesse says is always the first which he recalls whenever he thinks of *The Idiot,* where Prince Myshkin—I am here following Hesse's reconstruction[6]—has received a visit from the entire Epanchin family a few days after an epileptic attack. Suddenly a group of young revolutionaries and nihilists come into this lively and elegant circle. On the one side stand the elegant people of the world, the rich, powerful and conservative, and on the other side the raging youth, implacable, thinking of nothing but tearing down, knowing nothing but their hate for the traditional. Between these two parties the Prince, alone, speaks, regarded critically and with highest tension by both sides. And how does this scene end? By the Prince offending both sides, and being rejected by both sides, not by one party or the other, not perhaps by the young in opposition to the old, or the other way around, but by both, by both! For one moment the most extreme opposites in society, age, and attitude are totally erased, and all are united, fully united in turning away from him.

---

[6] *Blick ins Chaos,* pp. 23 f.

Who is this that is so incomparably lonely in the midst of people? What sort of a standpoint is that on which he seems to wish to stand outside all other standpoints? From where does this enigma think, speak, observe, and what is the goal toward which he is moving? What kind of unknown position is that which can be described only as the comprehensive opposite to all known positions? What kind of meaning is that which appears only as the non-meaning of all else that is called meaning? And what kind of knowledge of life is this which takes its source from the moment of death? With those questions we stand immediately before the secret of *The Idiot*, or even already in the midst of it, for these questions are their own answers. He is concerned with a final abrogation of life on final grounds. Because none of the many positions on earth is large, wide, and deep enough to include in itself that final ground that is the ground of everything, and with which he is concerned, he can therefore point to this one only when he again and again abrogates the others. Because he is searching for the eternal standpoint of God, he must therefore again and again pass by all human standpoints. Because he is not content with any of the many provisional answers and solutions by which men avoid the equivocal nature of life, the ever-renewed discovery of this infinite, equivocal nature itself is therefore his strange, lonely task. Because children are near to him in this, since they have not yet gone beyond the astonishment, amazement, and dread of the magnitude, fearfulness, and enigmatic nature of life, he is therefore able to get along so well with children. "To a child you can say everything, everything! How well the children realize that their parents think they are too little and too dumb to understand, when they actually understand everything!" That is certainly spoken in a sense very different from a pedagogical one! So it comes to this strange accomplishment of life as the Idiot lives it. Of a life in which the

whole equivocal nature of all life breaks out like a disease
and cries for healing, of a life in which therefore nothing
remains in balance, because everything points beyond itself,
strives forward toward a *final* answer and truth. This cor-
responds to the totally paradoxical, humanly speaking, completely impossible attitude which the Idiot assumes. His
problem which arose in the search for final answers finds its
adequate expression in that all of life becomes problematical,
as Dostoevsky has depicted it with such unprecedented artistry
in this figure.

Thus also in the case of the Idiot it is a matter of the in-
effable nature of life, of God's mystery, which Raskolnikoff
undertook to probe, and toward which the Karamazovs pressed
in the ardor of their passions. With his endless questioning
he seeks to press through to the source of life. In this he is
like Raskolnikoff and the Karamazovs. But he is different from
them in that he knows what they do not know, but must
learn through torment and suffering, that this source cannot
be found on earth, but is to be found in *God,* that it *is* God.
Therefore he does not try to touch it, or undertake Promethean attempts to try to express the inexpressible, as does
Raskolnikoff, or to give it an earthly name, form, and appearance as the Karamazovs do. He, too, knows of the love for
woman and the beauty of women and the fullness of their
spell as well as does Mitya Karamazov. "A wonderful face!"
he cries out on seeing the portrait of a seductive woman, and
presses it excitedly to his lips. And, moreover, when he tries
to speak of that ultimate, great, inexpressible, of the divine
which motivates him, and of which we can speak only in
pictures and parables, then beauty serves him for a comparison, because he sees it in its earthly splendor especially
full of the intimations of that inexpressible other that he
wants to speak about. "Beauty," he says in an important
passage, "will redeem the world." But it remains for him

intimation, picture, parable. It never becomes for him the matter itself. He celebrates no Olympian springtime with it. He does not let it seduce him to dreams of deification. He is already standing there where those others, those great deceived ones, finally end, in the judgment and light of that "new outlook" of Raskolnikoff, in the humbly strong yearning of Mitya Karamazov for resurrection.

So *he* is the true continuation of Raskolnikoff and the unwritten part of the story of the Karamazovs, although he precedes them in time. He never disturbs the boundaries of the last things, and never shortens the eternal distances. But he guards them. He is always seeking with all the power of his soul that ultimate point where everything has its end and its beginning in God, that ultimate point which is comparable only with death and birth. It is from that point that he thinks and speaks, or at least out of his striving to attain that point. There is the root of the "supreme rationality of this idiot," as his enemy and friend Rogozhin once says, "which is greater and better than all the others put together, who have not even dreamed of such a rationality." With this he proclaims his God. Yes, that is the highest, the truly positive, that can be said of him; his true secret is that he makes *God* known. Not through specific words or actions, but because all his words and all his actions are in a totally indescribable manner full of indications of the meaning and origin of life in God. It is always as if he were trying to discover in all men and all things the traces of the original creation and the secret tendency toward resurrection that is within them.

In a totally incomparable way this comes out in his relation to Nastasia, in whose form he encounters woman. Perhaps the power of beauty to seduce in defiance of all obstacles is depicted more powerfully in this woman than in Grushenka. "With such beauty one could turn the world upside down," it was said of her. Here it becomes quite clear what the erotic is when it no longer points beyond itself; it is the attempt of man to become like God, and therefore, in as far as he succeeds, the most powerful, truly demonic embodiment of the Fall. But just that—insofar as he succeeds! For even here he is not able to succeed entirely. In the midst of the noisy feast of love, despite all the singing and laughter the cracking of the glass is audible, and the approaching crisis is visible in the quiet, ultimate uncertainty of man. From the very first the Prince saw in Nastasia's features this final throbbing of the heart that betrays uncertainty. "A wonderful face," he said, "but in this face is much torment." And hot compassion flames up in him. He loves her with this compassion. He loves her for the sake of the secret disharmony in her soul, for this disharmony hints of bondage, and bondage hints of redemption. She is, however, compelled by just this compassionate love, more compelled than by all the passion that Rogozhin lavishes on her.

It is as if here the magic of the erotic must give way before a stronger magic, for in this compassionate love it is not only woman, but mankind in woman, that feels reached and understood. "The prince?" asks Nastasia. "He is the first person I have met in my life for whom I have really felt affection. At the first glance he believed in me, and so I also believe in him." All this does not result in reformation. Nastasia remains what she is and goes on her demonic way to the end. Here, too, the ultimate solution is never made visible as a human possibility for the ordering of life alongside other possibilities. Here, too, only negative features indicate its presence. But it only becomes all the clearer that the light, the *invisible* and *unearthly* light of a great *forgiveness* that is spread out in this book over all the errors and follies of men, is truly the light of *God*.

Forgiveness, the forgiveness of sins. Perhaps this is the right word to express the deepest meaning of the solution, the solution and interpretation of all the confusion of life, which is already represented by Alyosha and the starets in *The Brothers Karamazov,* and which Dostoevsky wishes to bring to light as such here in *The Idiot.* To be sure, this precious word is so much abused that it would almost be better to leave it unexpressed. But here it may for once be in its proper place, and all the more so since it so clearly points to something to which, according to Dostoevsky's own witness, the profound problem of this book should point, to *Christ.*

Exactly at this point the essential connection of Dostoevsky's knowledge with the ultimate knowledge of the Bible is unmistakable.

III | Dostoevsky's Perspective

We will cease conjuring up more and more figures from the world of Dostoevsky. We have seen enough to be able to see what we must see. We came to Dostoevsky with the question of man, and he answered us by returning our question in the picture of a man who is himself nothing but a single great question, the question of the origin of his life, the question of God. How could we in any better or different way summarize the impression of the powerful line which must be recognized as decisive, the careful delineation in the portrayals of *Crime and Punishment, The Brothers Karamazov,* and *The Idiot*? We have called the problem of *The Idiot* a life problem which arose in the search for ultimate answers. And that is essentially the picture that we receive from all of Dostoevsky's figures, *his* picture of man. These people all seem sick, as from a secret wound, from the deep, penetrating question of their lives, which they are unable to answer until they finally find their true recovery in their sickness, because in this sickness they perceive the meaning of life in an ultimate question. For where there is an ultimate question there is also an ultimate answer. How else should there be a question concerning it? It is only in the question that man can get hold of this ultimate answer, however, because it is an *ultimate* answer. But in this he *does* get hold of it. Thus they all stand before us as the great questioners, as those who point beyond themselves, imprisoned in the storms of their passions, in the entanglements of their thoughts, in the struggles of their dialogues, moved and oppressed by something unspeakably great, distant, and yet near, something beyond and yet here. In this, willingly or unwillingly they are God's messengers and martyrs, his prisoners, his heralds. Questioning, they themselves are questioned and give the answer. Seeking, they themselves are sought for and found. Pointing beyond, hinting at something inexpressibly great and distant, they are signs and proofs of his presence.

> Thou hast beset me behind and before,
>   and laid thine hand upon me.
> If I ascend up into heaven, thou art there:
>   if I make my bed in hell, behold, thou art there.
>   (Ps. 139:5, 8, K.J.V.)

The endlessness of their passion for the endlessness of that life which is promised to them is testimony; the greatness of their oppression by the greatness of the oppressor is the message. "Arrows of longing for the other shore" (Nietzsche). They themselves have been sent from there, sent by the unknown God. He who has ears to hear, let him hear! These are Dostoevsky's men and women.

But are they only *his* men and women? We are all acquainted with the mistrustful rejection of these figures of Dostoevsky as "Russian men and women." We would like to think that we are far away from those people, who, as we say, are so fantastically exaggerated, always rising to heaven and plunging to hell, always caught in metaphysical spasms, oppressed and devastated, and we would like to think of them as confined (together with Lenin and Bolshevism) to that enigmatic distant land over there in the East, beyond all western borders, from whence they once came to us as strangers.

There are those among us who, in contrast to these presentations, are glad to appeal to the "healthier food" of Jeremias Gotthelf's writings, which are, or seem to be, so much friendlier. The remarkable thing here is that as a rule the same persons who reject Dostoevsky's "unhealthy distortions" are just as offended by the unprecedented *realism* of his presentations of people as they are by the "distortions" they observe. From this observation we may take the indication that there is perhaps really an inner connection between these two things, a connection between the humanity of Dostoevsky's men and women, which he depicts with that unprecedented realism for which he is known, and their equally questionable, continual soaring into the beyond, their progress toward eternity. Perhaps the whole meaning of the interpretation of man which Dostoevsky represents lies exactly here in the polarity of these two designations. Those fastidious persons who reject Dostoevsky may be therefore more right than they imagine when they turn away from the inhuman-supraworldly as much as from the all-too-human earthly in Dostoevsky. For it is quite possible that the one is determined by the other.

It is questionable, however, it should be said, whether they can turn with more right to Jeremias Gotthelf. Perhaps there is slumbering in his words a message that will one day clang fearfully in the ears of those who want to find in him only homeland and a pastoral theology. In reality there is not so great a distance (taken with a grain of salt) between the seemingly wholesome Bern of Jeremias Gotthelf and the Russia of Dostoevsky as might be surmised from the geographical distance. In any case Gottfried Keller runs more danger of being too "healthy" then Jeremias Gotthelf does. Perhaps it is only that what is intimated in the deeper stories of Jeremias Gotthelf breaks forth in the great creations of Dostoevsky.

But enough of these side-glances. We are concerned here

with the observation that this march of men over and out beyond all that is human is found in Dostoevsky in a picture of man which is indisputably drawn with ultimate realism. Therefore it is possible to claim realism even for this march to the Infinite. In any case it is no longer possible to ignore it and omit it from the picture of the men and women of Dostoevsky. It is not one feature among many, and one which could under certain circumstances be omitted. It is rather precisely the characteristic, the essential, the specific feature and direction of all his work. Dostoevsky himself was well aware of this essential connection between realism and transcendent definiteness in his characters. "Find the *human* in man by absolute realism," is the way he himself once described the inmost tendency of his art. Thus it is really not only national peculiarities that he depicts for us, and his Russian is really not only the *Russian* man. There is therefore inherent in life itself, the whole of life, all life, to a greater extent than we realize, that unprecedented march over "toward the other shore." Thus not only in the East, but also in the West this hunger and thirst for the eternal, this passion for the Infinite, is the essential trait of man. Therefore we discover, and the more so as we take life realistically, something mysteriously *un*real, and the deeper we delve into the earthly, something powerfully *un*earthly at the basis of all things, until finally all of life begins to burn before our eyes, as in Dostoevsky, with the one great question, the question of the unknown God.

Perhaps here one more side-glance may be permitted. We are thinking of the remarkable, elongated, and animated figures in the paintings of *El Greco,* or the variously attacked creations of the *Expressionists,* which are often with good reason compared to Dostoevsky's work. The obvious dislocations and distortions of these figures can hardly be due to defective vision, as some have surmised for El Greco. Most probably these painters also have seen something of that deep tendency of life toward the beyond. "This mortal must put on immortality" (I Cor. 15:53). But it may be here that artistic impossibilities are present, over which it is possible to hold divergent opinions in good faith. Rather, let us remember that the correctness of the most commonly and generally accepted drawing depends on that relationship of all lines to a single point of view that lies outside the picture, on that relationship that is called perspective. Not some fantastic addition or grotesque exaggeration, but rather just such a strict and exact relationship of all lines to a vanishing point in the beyond is what we mean by that course toward the beyond and toward infinity which we have recognized as characteristic of Dostoevsky's men and women. When we call the polarity between his realism and his tendency to the beyond the inmost secret of his art, we intend nothing else than such a connection between the vanishing point and each single line of the picture, which guarantees the truth of the representation.

It is usual to regard Dostoevsky as the *psychologist* par excellence among the artists. He may be called that. But then his whole psychology is a psychology that is one no longer, because it continuously negates itself, for the final result of all penetrating analyses of man is the confirmation of that thoroughly *synthetic* relationship of all that is human to a vanishing point that lies beyond the whole of psychological reality. The whole picture of life which is given by this psychology which is no longer psychology points on out beyond itself to this vanishing point. It was undoubtedly in recognition of this fact that Dostoevsky himself rejected the title of psychologist. "I am called a psychologist, but that is not correct. I am only a realist in a higher sense, that is, I reveal all the depths of the soul of man," he once said of himself. And in *The Brothers Karamazov* he characterizes with ironic emphasis as "a good psychologist, with claim to know the human soul particularly well" one of those haughty jurists who have no inkling of the true depths of the soul of the accused.

Would it be better to number Dostoevsky, with his "higher realism," among the metaphysicians? That, too, has already been done, and he may be called one if necessary. But if he is, then his metaphysics is in any case, in the strict sense of the word, a *transcendental* metaphysics which does not take any material principles into consideration. And the other world of which he is always speaking is no concrete upper world, or even an unknown, spiritual underworld. For that which is the presupposition, the basis, and the essential determinant for all cannot in turn be itself something determinate or determinable, any more than the viewpoint of the perspective is a real point lying somewhere within the picture. It is called an imaginary point. It is unreal, imaginary, that is, it is that external, ultimate point in the beyond, the point which does not lie in any psychological depth, however fine and concealed, nor in any ideal height of the historic-psychological reality, and by which Dostoevsky sees that all of human life is determined. For this point of all points is *God*.

God is *God*. That is the one, central recognition of truth for Dostoevsky. His only concern is not to permit this God to become a man-god, no matter in what heights his throne may be, nor a piece of the reality of human soul or of the world, no matter how idealistic.

Here at last we have attained the height of the problem Dostoevsky dealt with. The question of *God* is *the* question of all his works: God, the root of all life, and the basis of the world, which gives everything its basis, but also its abrogation, its torment, its "dis-ease," the enigmatically unreal in all that is real, the unearthly, toward which all that is earthly aspires. The dialectic of this paradoxical truth is the dialectic of all

Dostoevsky's men and women. They all have God as their goal, they are all moved and driven by him from the beginning on. They press toward him in the insatiability of their longing for life, in the search for final answers, and yet *no* step leads over from man, for how would God still be God if *man* could become god? So again and again all attempts to storm heaven fail, and as the meaning of life there remains only the gigantic, eschatological tension of this problem itself. It is there from the first page of his books and remains to their close. Already in the first hasty strokes in which he draws the external traits of his heroes, their appearances, and the exposition of their actions, there is found the whole riddle of their humanity, which cries out for redemption, and the development of the riddle forms the whole further content of the book.

They all travel on a road without beginning or end. Various things happen on the way, many things, great, even terrible things, and yet each time at the conclusion the reader asks, what has really happened? Has something changed? Has a happy solution of difficult riddles been found? Has society been renewed? Or at least have ways for its renewal been found and displayed? Have devils become angels, or at least, have men become saints? And again and again the answer is the same, nothing like that has happened! At the end no end has been reached. Afterwards as before, society is questionable and corrupt, and the individuals are questionable and one-sided. At the end there are no matured, enlightened, purified personalities standing before us as there are in the famous developmental novels of German literature. Rather the opposite has happened. Siberian prisons are at the end of *Crime and Punishment* and *The Brothers Karamazov.* Stavrogin, one of the heroes in *The Possessed,* hangs himself on the last page of the book, and the Idiot goes back again to his nerve clinic. And yet, something has happened, something has changed! The questionability of everything human has become greater, and now with truly shattering power the problem of all being cries out for its final solution in God. That is the result!

Once more, if it were otherwise, the solution would not lie in *God*. Precisely because it is in *God*, and *only* in him, the final word of true knowledge of life can therefore be nothing else than the question about him. Where this question is raised most vigorously, there the meaning of life becomes apparent in the greatest clarity. When this is recognized, however, then beyond this final word an absolutely final word may be spoken boldly: God would certainly not be God, if he were not really the solution. And therefore the problematical does not remain the final word of true knowledge of life. Behind it an absolutely final word can be perceived. What is impossible for men is possible for God. If no path leads from us over to him, then all the more certainly a path leads from him to us. *Revelation* is proclaimed here! In Dostoevsky the eschatological tension develops into eschatology itself. The absolutely final word of his novels is "resurrection." Over the dark abysses of the humanity which he depicts there glows from the beyond the light of a great *forgiveness*. His men and women confront the problematical nature of their lives questioning, crushed and broken, vexed and shaken. It looms over them like the nearness of death. It is not accidental that a pair of dying men, the starets in *The Brothers Karamazov* and the old man of God and pilgrim Makar Ivanovitch in *The Adolescent*, lead the way. But in their death is a new birth, "rebirth," as it is called in *Crime and Punishment*. In their being crushed there is "transition from one world into another" (*Crime and Punishment*), in their questioning, "acquaintance with a new, previously unknown reality" (*Crime and Punishment*). At no time and in no place do they stand there with any sort of firm solution and answer in their hands.

But they stand in the light of the unprecedented *hope* that salvation *is coming* from *God's* hands.

Certainly these insights and words are absolutely final words and insights. The unprecedented moment, into the light of which these crushed and broken men, these murderers and harlots and convicts, have entered, where the tension of the problematical nature of life is released by *God*, where the viewpoint and the lines of the picture which are in relation to him (*horribile dictu*) flow together, this moment signifies the end of the picture altogether, and is therefore for those who are themselves in the picture no longer a thought that can be fully formed, nor an experience (unless it is the experience of death), and it has nothing in common with any of those moments of temporal elevation and enlightenment of the man who would like to undertake on his own to get rid of the eschatological tension of his life by making himself a god, and preparing for himself an Olympian festival. Dostoevsky's works are full of proclamation, full of suggestion of that absolutely final turning to the transformation of everything on earth, to the breaking forth of ultimate answers to truly eternal life removed from all that is problematical. But they do not go beyond suggestion and proclamation. To want more would be to want less. Dostoevsky is no romantic. There is nothing against which he defended himself more vigorously for the sake of the purity, the significance, and the power of this *final* turning than against all attempts to make again out of this final, eternal moment a pre-final one, to make out of this exclusively *divine* possibility again a *human* possibility that could be depicted. To attempt this is to tempt God. Dostoevsky, however, knew that this attempt is a temptation for man, the one most powerful temptation that threatens his whole humanity and his whole relation to the beyond. He wrestled with it all his life, as with his most dreadful foe. His heroes never appear except as fighters in the midst of the mighty entanglements of this struggle. And it is not merely for the sake of a literary contrast that in all his works the Hosanna rings forth only out of the depths of the most dreadful insurrection. All his knowledge of man lies in these opposites and pairs of opponents. As deeply characteristic for human life as man's creaturely relation to God is, so deeply characteristic is also his not recognizing this ultimate relationship, his Promethean rebellion against it.

Let us look back once more. Why must Prince Myshkin be an idiot? Because all human wisdom, everything that passes for a view of life or of the world among us is nothing else but the attempt to escape the question (as question!) about God, while not to avoid it but to face it squarely is the divine folly of the Idiot. Why does this Idiot gain his deepest knowledge out of the moment of death? Why does Alyosha hear from the mouth of a dying man the fullness of his insight and of his loving understanding of all sin and folly? Why is it indeed that again and again a couple of dying men are the ones who truly know and understand in Dostoevsky's works? It is because the dying are especially near the great shadow of the absolute enigma that lies over existence as the most urgent witness that the meaning of life is not to be found in this life. Again and again in their blindness the living seek it there; the dying have become wise.

Why is the young Alyosha, with all his faith and his redemptive insights, able to move only on the edge of the world of the Karamazovs? Because in the middle of the Karamazovs' world, as of every world, disbelief rules, the "dark catechism," as it is called in *Crime and Punishment,* that man is god, and that everything is permitted to him. Why must the harlot Sonia, a simple, humiliated girl, be the one who reveals to the murderer Raskolnikoff the deep meaning of his life through the story of the resurrection of Lazarus?

Because all others are determined to avoid that sickness of life for God, and in their own way to remain strong, healthy, and powerful, and therefore also are unable to know anything of resurrection and rebirth.

Why was it deliberately so that the constantly drunken father of that harlot, sitting in a cellar saloon, should tell of the forgiveness on the last day in the ecstatic words: "But he will have compassion on us, he who has compassion on all, and who understands everyone and everything; he is the only one, and he is also the judge. On that day he will speak to us: 'You come too,' he will say. 'Come you drunkards, come you weaklings, come you sinners!' And we will all come before him without shame, and will stand there. And then he will say, 'You swine! You images of animals! You with ox-like faces, you come too!' And the wise and clever ones will call out, 'Lord, why do you accept them?' And he will say, 'I accept them, you clever ones, I accept them, you wise ones, because not one of them thought he was worthy.' . . . And he will hold his hands out to us, and we will sink down . . . and will weep . . . and understand all! . . . Then we will understand all. . . . Lord, thy kingdom come!" The answer to our questions lies in the words themselves. Because forgiveness is *not* proclaimed by the wise and the clever, by the pious and the righteous, therefore the very stones cry out; because it has been forgotten in the churches, it rings forth in the streets. Because men have become clever, righteous, wise, and pious *without* God, therefore God stands in a corner of the earth and is seen and understood only by those who have been cast out and disinherited, by those who are depraved and corrupt.

That is the rebellion of man against God. With that keen-sightedness of ultimate, penetrating knowledge of life and insight into life, Dostoevsky recognized this tendency to revolt, this darkening of the eyes to the true meaning of life, precisely here in the *most positive* accomplishments of man.

This is the reason for his deep, critical distrust of culture and society. He did not see in it merely this or that which was distorted or in need of improvement. He sensed in all its proud towers and battlements the tower of Babel, the deep-rooted tendency of man to make himself at home in the world without God and against God, as a god himself, the attempt to produce a picture and form of life while omitting any consideration of that ultimate, other-worldly vanishing point of all life in God. Senselessness, fearful shattering, and collapse must be the necessary result and end of such a culture that is falsely oriented internally and rejects God. Dostoevsky continually prophesied a sea of blood for Europe.

Above all, in unequivocal manner he held a mirror up before the eyes of the *bourgeoisie*, the spiritual upholders of this culture. Nowhere, not even in Tolstoy, is the inner decay, deceit, and instability of the so-called good society made so fearsomely apparent as in all the novels of Dostoevsky. Every moral criticism that socialism brought against the ruling class was already depicted in Dostoevsky. We have only to think of the erotic orgies that he describes. We should also reflect that he hardly even once speaks of a completely unobjectionable, normal middle-class marriage (and who would dare to insist that he saw wrongly!). We can hear the weeping and sobbing of children, which is suppressed and yet continually breaking forth, and which in Dostoevsky's work constantly appears as the sole witness to the upbringing of children in this society that is so proud of its upbringing and so enlightened. This gives notice of the agonizing unnaturalness that is hidden behind its glitering facades. All the questioning and the astonished, frightened, and embittered childish eyes, which throughout Dostoevsky's work are fixed on the deeds of the adults like a dreadful, immanent critique, seem to cry out a great "We see through it all!" Again and again the root out of which all the corruption arises is not this or that separate moral failing, but the complete refusal to come to know the deepest, ultimate, other-worldly relationship of life, the obviously compounded self-deification, in which these men of society pursue their policy of "everything goes."

The totally radical nature of his critique, however, is seen in that it also strikes socialism with the utmost severity, socialism that would bring a counterattack within society, end middle-class culture, and proclaim a new society. Even there, yes, there most of all, Dostoevsky sees the titantic countenance of the man who, as it says in *The Brothers Karamazov*, would "erect the fearsome tower of Babel," who would establish "an eternal life in this world" (a flagrant *contradictio in adjecto!*). Not that Dostoevsky was in the least concerned with the existing order; because of its corruption it has earned its destruction ten times over. The eternal word against it has already been spoken. Kierkegaard's words apply to it: "When authority and power are once misused in the world and have brought the nemesis of revolution on themselves, they actually have been only impotence and weakness, which, wishing to stand on their own feet, brought this nemesis on themselves."[7] "Anyway, refer to the Apocalypse," says Dostoevsky in this connection in *The Adolescent*. Still, he sees the lack of order and power, the arbitrariness and self-glorification, in a word, the revolts against God, the "insubordination" (*The Brothers Karamazov*) which inhere in human revolutions. In the social structure of the new society which might proceed from the revolution, in the "huge, conformist ant hill" of democracy, he sensed only renewed monstrosity and new idolatry. He ascertained the nonsense in wishing to bring in a new time and a new humanity through streams of blood,

---

[7] Quoted by Theodore Haecker in *Brenner*, 1920, vol. 7.

"through chopping off a hundred million heads" (*The Possessed*). And he was equally repulsed by the dogma of the "evolution of gorilla to superman" (*The Possessed*), as the great blasphemy which was at the basis of the middle-class socialism of liberal reform. A singular, impassioned novel, *The Possessed*, is dedicated to dealing with these issues.

He saw an especially potent germ of destruction in the *materialistic science* and world view which was equally recognized and practiced by both sides, by the middle-class and by the socialists. According to his view, they essentially represent the attempt, the foolish and yet so infinitely clever attempt, to eliminate all traces of the other-worldly from this world, of the unearthly from the earthly. He pours over them copious streams of irony and polemic.

Yet the most fearsome attack which Dostoevsky led with the assembled power of his knowledge and all the passion of his heart was directed against *religion and the church*. This attack runs through all his works, but reaches its high point in "The Grand Inquisitor," and in Ivan Karamazov's nightmare of the devil.

IV | Ivan Karamazov, the Grand Inquisitor, and the Devil

Again we see the attempt, by turning the God who is other-worldly and unknown into one who is this-worldly and known, to escape that deeply problematical feature of life, in which alone the God who is beyond can and will attest himself to man. This is the attempt which Dostoevsky detected in religion and the church. Man finds his creatureliness unbearable, the relationship (and the negation that accompanies it) of his entire visible life to the eternal, invisible creation of God, standing under God's judgment, lying on God's scales. And he seeks to be rid of his God by gaining control of him. The vanishing point in the beyond is shoved into the picture; God himself becomes a component part of the spiritual and historical reality of man, and with that he becomes *God-no-longer,* an idol. This is the really dangerous revolt, the "insurrection" against God, dangerous because it takes place, not in open resistance, with a willful ignoring of God, but in his name, and even while calling on him.

The presentation and explication of this insurrection of man against God in religion and church is the content and meaning of the famous "Story of the Grand Inquisitor" told by Ivan in *The Brothers Karamazov.*

Let us consider it.

In the story, which follows the course of the threefold temptation of Jesus by the devil, Christ stands on the one side and has nothing in his hands except—as Dostoevsky says meaningfully—"freedom," that is, an other-worldly, paradoxical basing of life on God, which finds expression in making all of life problematical. This problematic, which God gives to man in order to show that he *is* God, is threefold. Man must be able to stand in a threefold tension if he would be true to the deepest meaning of his life.

1. He must be able to deny himself "bread," earthly satisfaction, individual and collective earthly happiness, the kingdom of God on *earth*, that "eternal life in this world," as it is called in another passage. For "man does not live by bread alone." The meaning of life does not lie in *this* life, but in God. From this comes all the deeply questionable and uncertain nature of this life, the limitation of the temporal and finite existence of man here and now. All problematical attempts to bring "fire down from heaven" end of necessity with the great disappointment: "They who promised us the fire of heaven have not given it to us."[8] And each new "tower of Babel" "remains unfinished just like the first one." But it is precisely in the limits of his temporal and finite nature, in this earthly part of him, in that final, invincible dullness and lowliness of his physical basis that man finds life full of allusions to God and his "other-worldly" possibilities, his "heavenly bread." Man must therefore accept this questionable and uncertain nature of his being for the sake of the allusions that it contains. He must accept it without tangible guarantees, with "empty hands," as Dostoevsky says, and follow these allusions, remain obedient to the other-worldly meaning of his life. He must accept the loss of his earthly security in order to win an entirely different security that is totally inconceivable to him.

Like Israel of old, he is again and again confronted by

---

[8] Unless otherwise noted, all quotations here and in the following pages are taken from the story of "The Grand Inquisitor" in *The Brothers Karamazov*.

the choice either to be immediately dependent on God himself, on God alone, on the unknown, other-worldly God (and does that not mean stepping out into the void?), or to be dependent then on his peers, on earthly gods, on kings or governments. Here he does not step out into the void; here there are tangible, visible idols; here bread and happiness are promised and passed out. There is "something that is no longer subject to doubt about its being worthy of worship," "something that *all* can at once worship directly," an earthly kingdom that is consequently only of *this* world, and we know what that means! This choice is the "freedom" of man. He who decides for God takes the leap from the ground of human surety off into the dark. To wish to have it some other way would be to sell your birthright for a mess of pottage. "For what kind of freedom is that, if obedience is bought with bread?" the Grand Inquisitor says to Christ. What kind of God is that to whom man is true in any way but unconditionally and to the utmost? But who dares accept this new and fearful, this boundless, kingly freedom? Who dares take the leap into the dark? Who dares accept God?

2. But it is not only happiness that man may *not* count on in this world, insofar as he understands his position in relation to God. He may not even count on the security of his *spiritual* existence. He must comprehend that this other-worldly meaning which his life has can in every respect appear to his this-worldly thinking and understanding only as the "non-sense" of his life. The leap into the dark is really a leap into the *dark*. The divine promise is *divine* promise in that it constantly stands over against all that is humanly attainable as completely inconceivable and extraordinary. Man can be true to the real meaning of his life only in those great negations of all human standpoints and possibilities which are at home in life (as we have seen it take place in *The Idiot*). How monstrous this demand is! For, Dostoevsky says, "with-

out a firm understanding of why he should live, man will never consent to live, but will rather destroy himself than to remain living on earth." So radical is this threat! In common with all others he wants something that he can worship, a firm conviction, a guaranteed world view; "firm bases for the stilling of human conscience once for all." But, please—no "miracles and impenetrable secrets," no riddles, "dark chasms and abysses," before which he could lose his inner peace and security! "But you," the Grand Inquisitor says reproachfully to Christ, "you chose everything uncommon, enigmatic, and indefinite that there is, everything that exceeds the powers of man." You place man before God, that is, in the most complete "freedom" from each and every visible, tangible, well-grounded, this-worldly, human, material principle of life. There where they all end, the divine begins. It is their crisis, their finish, or it is not divine. To enter into this "freedom," to leave behind all that is humanly determined, clear, certain, that is the utmost torment, "a fearsome burden." Christ lays this burden on men. Who can bear it?

3. And for a third time the ground is pulled from under man's feet, for now he must renounce God himself, that is to say, a God who is revealed to him other than in a great question, a God who appears to him elsewhere than out there on the edge of those abysses, where *everything* becomes problematical, a God whom he could behold elsewhere than out of the "purgatorial fires of doubt" and tribulation. For God himself cannot be substantiated or conceived in human terms. *Faith* begins only there where in the confirmations and concepts, confirmation and concept cease, all assurances and certainty end. But man calls out for *"miracles."* That means, for the other-worldly relationship of his life to become visible, tangible, portrayable. He is unwilling to believe without seeing. Nevertheless, Christ denies him these "miracles." This is the only way it can be, for how should that which is other-

worldly become visible here? If it were visible, it would have already ceased to be other-worldly; a miracle that can be and is established is no longer a true miracle. The miracle that man demands and gets in his religions is the this-worldly miracle, the "miracle" that is one no longer, the "miracle" without God. No, Christ does *not* cast himself down from the pinnacle of the temple, and man, "in the moments of the fundamental, most fearsome and tormenting questions of his soul remains" directed toward "the free decision of his heart." The essence of faith is unconfirmability, pure other-worldliness, if it is faith in *God*. This faith itself is the sole true miracle. But where does this miracle take place?

That is the threefold tension in which man is placed. But he has not accepted this situation. He is unwilling to launch out with God. The demand is too great; it exceeds his powers. It is not so much that man seeks God, but rather that he seeks happiness and bread. He wants to know what he is to believe and do. He wants to believe in a God who is congenial to him, who can be conceived and substantiated. He cannot stand the atmosphere of that fearful "freedom." The *church* knows that, and she takes pity on him. She takes more pity and shows a much more tender, more understanding love than Christ himself. The church takes man's burden away, stands by his side and gives him what he needs; she promises, preaches, gives him that "childhood happiness," as Dosto-evsky calls it, which he would like to have. But all this, to be sure, at the price of his "freedom," that is, at the price of a betrayal of God, whom man can serve only in freedom. She promises man bread—on the condition that he will let himself be led by her *"authority"* (that is, no longer led directly by God himself). She looks out for firm, clear, def-inite goals for the conscience, for an ascertainable meaning of life, for a religious-social or middle-class ideology, for morals and the accompanying forgiveness of sins—on the condition

that the authentication of this ideology of life, of these ways
and goals of life, remain her own "secret" (that is, that the
meaning of all life now no longer lies in God alone). She
promises him signs and feelings of the divine presence, religious festivals, exaltation and experience—on the condition
that he believe in her "*miracles*" (that is, that he no longer
believe without seeing). "We have improved your work, and
built it on the basis of miracle, mystery, and authority," the
Grand Inquisitor says to Christ. That is the church's threefold
betrayal of God. She no longer leads man to that depth where
he is only able to cry out to God in the heights. But because
of this she no longer leads him there where God can show
himself to man as the God on high with great might, with his
true love, his *true* forgiveness, his *true* miracle. That is the
deceit, the godlessness of religion.

This powerful analysis of the essence of religion and
church receives, however, its ultimate pointedness in that it is
placed in the mouth of the demonic atheist Ivan Karamazov,
and is spoken, not as a critique of religion and church, but as
their justification. In full consciousness of what he is doing,
Ivan Karamazov justifies godlessness as religion and religion
as godlessness. His dialectic develops also in three stages. In
the novel itself these three stages are not distinguished from
one another in the sharp manner of the following analysis;
rather they are in part interwoven in various ways with one
another, and in part they are presented widely separated from
one another. In the following pages we shall attempt to see
their systematic development.

1. Ivan's thought begins with a passionate protest against
the reconciliation of the riddles and torments of life with the
divine order of the world that is asserted by religion. Frightful pictures are given of the torments of poor innocent children. The riddle of such torments, says Ivan, cannot be wiped
out by the splendidly conceived future harmony of the eternal

world. They may perhaps be atoned for, but they cannot be undone. The bill does not add up. "What can I do with revenge? What use are all the sufferings of sinners in hell to me, if the child has already been tortured to death?" And the atonement itself can only come about at the price of new tortures. "And where then is harmony if there is a hell? I want to pardon and embrace, and do not want any more suffering." But if we pardon and embrace, where then are atonement and retribution? "I need retribution, or I will destroy myself!" These opposites stand irreconcilably over against each other. The riddles of existence burn unquenchable, insoluble, and they demand their unknown solution in God, that harmony, totally different, which exceeds all thought, demand it as that by which religions and churches may comfort and console man. Who can show it to us? That is the protest of the atheist Ivan Karamazov.

But is the answer not already contained in this question so full of accusation? Because they cry out for a solution, the riddles and torments of life already proclaim the solution that transcends all thought. By crying out for the unknown God they are already bearing witness to him. Something inconceivably "precious" would have to "appear," Ivan says, "in order for it to be adequate for all hearts, for the quieting of all discontent, for the atonement of all horrors, not only for forgiveness, but also for the justification of all that has happened to man." Irreconcilable contradictions would have to become united in it. The insoluble accounting of life would have to be solved in it, and righteousness and love meet in it. Does this "precious thing" exist? Where is it? In any case it must lie beyond all human comprehension, like that infinite point where two parallel lines intersect. But this point cannot even be thought of without presumption, without violating the limits of thought. "How should I be able to conceive of God? That is indeed much too high for me. I have only a

Euclidean, an earthly, understanding, and how is it possible to judge about something that is not of this world?" That is the question of Ivan the atheist. But is it possible to speak of *God*, of the true God, more strongly, in any truer sense, than has been done in this atheistic question?

No, the original power of true knowledge of God is displayed in this atheism. The endless thirst for life of the Karamazov heart speaks in it, a thirst that cannot rest content with provisional, apparent answers, that senses and searches for the secret of the true, the unknown and inconceivable, other-worldly, eternal God beyond the comfort the church gives through the no-longer-God who has become only something to calm mankind. In the final analysis this atheism does not deny God. Its protest is directed rather to the church (which has succumbed to the second temptation) which by referring to God would like to silence the riddles of life, although it is precisely the riddles that witness to God because they cry out to God and refuse to be silenced.

The great, passionate negations of the false god make room once again for the knowledge of the true God. They seek to keep God and his eternal world from being made into something accessible to and comprehensible by the finite thought of man, his "Euclidean, earthly understanding," into a proof and an easy comfort with which men can deceive themselves into ignoring the riddles of life instead of listening to them. God is "nothing of this world." The vanishing point of the perspective is no real point within the picture. But again and again religion seeks on its own to include the other-worldly vanishing point in the picture, to judge about God, to operate with God, as if he were a part of this world. "They even have the audacity," says Ivan, "to think that two parallel lines, which according to Euclid can never under any circumstances intersect on earth, may perhaps intersect somewhere in infinity. They have the audacity to reckon with infinity as if it were a factor among others, found in some finite-human field. They have gained control of God, as if one could gain control of *God!*"

2. But now the inconceivable, the truly uncanny twist in the course of Ivan's thought from his dialectical, animated atheism to his metaphysically rigid, genuine, satanic atheism! This is the twist about which Dostoevsky himself later gave the following judgment: "The dolts who twit me for what they call my uncultured and old-fashioned belief in God have not even dreamed of such a denial of God as is expressed in my 'Grand Inquisitor' and the previous chapter, and to which the whole book gives answer." The same Ivan with his deep insight into the godlessness of religion, into the secret of the true God, the same Ivan who realized so sharply that basically man only uses his theodicies in order to resist boldly the inconceivable nature of the true God, in order to gain control of him, that same Ivan now himself confesses "with the power of Karamazov baseness" in cold blood, precisely this "bold step." "See," he says to Alyosha at the beginning of their conversation, "in the seventeenth century there lived a great sinner who said of God, *'s'il n'existait pas, il faudrait l'inventer.'* (If he did not exist he would have to be invented.) And in fact, man has invented his god." Ivan expresses admiration of this as "something that brings great honor to man," that such a thought—the thought of the indispensability of God—could enter the head of such a wild and evil animal as man, and then continues, "As for myself, I have determined not to reflect anymore whether man made God or God made man." He cynically rejects his deeper insight; "I declare that I accept God (that is, the conceivable, all-too-well-known, no-longer-God who has been dispossessed by man) simply and unhesitatingly."

In order that there may be no further doubt about this powerful twist, there follows immediately on this blasphe-

mous affirmation of the false god the not less blasphemous
denial of the true, other-worldly God, who is sovereign precisely in his inconceivableness, who does not need and is not
accessible to any human theodicy, and of the victorious harmony of his eternal world, which exists beyond all the contradictions and riddles of this world. He is denied explicitly,
and despite the fact that Ivan's deepest heart so passionately
yearns for the secret of *this* God. It is in spite of the knowledge
that only here before the absolute unsearchableness of God's
ways, only in the secret of his choosing and rejecting, once
more all insurrection against him, together with all theodicies,
all opposition, will be silent; the denial took place although
this knowledge was dawning on Ivan and was the power of
the protest with which he had turned against all human attempts at harmonizing as blasphemous.

He now explicitly rejects this secret of the true God; "For
myself, I am convinced that the hurt will form a scar and then
become smooth, that the whole sorrowful comedy of human
contradictions will disappear like a miserable phantom, like a
loathsome discovery of a weak, human, Euclidean understanding the size of an atom, and that finally at the end of the
world, in the moment of eternal harmony, something so
precious will appear that it will be adequate for all hearts,
for the stilling of all dissent, for the atonement of all blood
that has been spilt, that will be adequate not only for the forgiveness, but also for the justification of all that has happened
to man." Once more, is it possible to speak truer words of God
and of the victory of his justice and love? But is it possible to
end with greater blasphemy than there is in these words:
"Yes, yes, that may all very well be, but *I do not accept it and
do not intend to accept it,* not even if the parallel lines meet."
That is to say, even if God, the inconceivable, true God,
really exists! "And even if I see it myself, see it and say that
they have met" (that is, even though the absolute miracle of

faith really took place in me!), "I still will not accept it." And in the midst of the conversation, directly after the protest about the innocent suffering of children, which is nothing but a great cry to the unknown God and his unsearchable righteousness, a cry full of knowledge of God, this knowledge is once more denied with the words: "I realize how great the convulsion of the universe will be when everything in heaven, on earth, and under the earth joins in a single song of praise, when everything that is living or has lived cries out, 'Righteous art Thou, O Lord, for now thy ways are manifest!'" ... but "I *want* no harmony; I would rather remain in my unsilenceable wrath, *even if I were not right.*"

"That is insolent rebellion!" says Alyosha. That is the most fearsome, inflexible metaphysical atheism. Again and again this atheism of Ivan Karamazov, the burning passion in the depths of his heart for God, breaks through the thick cover like a suppressed fire. But again and again it is repressed by his invincible "proud decision," the decision for unbelief. This unprecedented conversation is carried on under the great tension of this struggle.

As the basis of his "I will not," "I *wish* no harmony," as the basis of his conscious denial of God, Ivan Karamazov tells here the story of "The Grand Inquisitor," who is none other than Ivan himself, who sacrifices to the false God all his deep insights about the true God. Why? "Out of love, love for mankind," which cannot stand the air of true worship of God and therefore needs false worship in its religions and churches. With the uncommon wisdom of his understanding, the Grand Inquisitor perceives the total immensity of the venture which is called *faith*, and will not expect man to take this venture, this leap into the dark, because he knows all too well what a weak and fearful creature man is. That is the meaning of the tale of "The Grand Inquisitor," which reveals once more the deep unbelief, the insolent rebellion against God, that inheres in religions and churches, but reveals it only to defend, to justify, to affirm it.

In the riddle of this self-contradiction, however, lies, without the Grand Inquisitor Ivan Karamazov knowing it, an apology of faith which is more profound and truer than all the apologies of its defenders in all ages.

3. The final consequence, however, of this twist of thought to rigid atheism is demonic, satanic. The Grand Inquisitor is the devil, who tempts Christ. Ivan Karamazov is the Grand Inquisitor. Therefore Ivan Karamazov is the devil. And so now we have that gruesome monologue of Ivan Karamazov with the devil at the close of the book. What else is the devil except the spirit who knows about God, the true, other-worldly God, not merely the man-god, and who still refuses to know of him! What else is the devil except the embodiment of the lie of an existence that was created to be in relationship with God and in titanic delusion seeks self-deification. He betrays his own deepest principles, and far from God serves the self-created sham god of his religions. The oscillating between hypocritical piety and cynically presumptuous self-deification is then also the characteristic of this conversation with the devil. "My only obsession," says the devil to Ivan, "is to embody myself in some fat shopkeeper's wife who weighs two hundred and fifty pounds, and believe in everything she believes in. It is my ideal to go to church and there with all my heart to be able to light a candle before a saint." And at the same time, "If mankind once completely breaks away from God, then the former world view, and above all, the former morality will collapse entirely of itself. . . . Man's spirit will raise itself in divine, titanic pride, and then the man-god will appear." In one and only one place in the conversation the question about God himself comes up. "Is there a God, or is there none?" Ivan suddenly cried with animal fury. "Oh, are you asking that seriously?" the devil

answered. "My dear sir, by God, I do not know." Ivan continued, "You don't know, and yet you see God?" And he adds,
"No, you do not exist in yourself, you are me, you are me and
nothing else!"

That is Ivan as we have learned to know him, the one who
knows about God and does not want to know about him. The
not wishing to know what one nevertheless knows, the not
wanting to see the question about God, in which nonetheless
life burns, that is the devilishness that makes life hell. For
what else is hell except life, this life, insofar as it is deceived
about its relationship to God? Thereby it loses its meaning.
It becomes a monstrosity, a lie, insanity; all its lines fall apart
like the lines of a picture that has lost its vanishing point. Not
in vain do a pair of huge, grotesque, gigantic *liars* stride
through Dostoevsky's works. We will mention only Lebedyev
and General Ivolgin in *The Idiot*. The preposterousness of
their lies exceeds all measure. But Dostoevsky knows what he
is doing when he has them lie to that extent. They are representatives of a humanity that has forgotten the truth of life,
representatives of a society that has become a lie, representatives of a world that is on its way to hell.

So then here, too, hell is portrayed as this our world, as
the world and the life of men, with merchants and their two
hundred and fifty pound wives, with priests and scholars,
doctors and tribunals. "Everything that there is with you is
also here with us. . . . *Satanas sum et nihil humani a me
alienum puto*" (I am Satan and I regard nothing human as
alien to me), the devil says to Ivan. Thus it is the same world,
only completely stripped of its own relations and determina-
tions. The same life, only wholly robbed of its responsiveness
to God and its movement toward God, which has come to rest
before reaching the goal and therefore is without goal. Therefore it has the most boring senselessness and the most senseless boredom. "This earth has perhaps repeated itself already

a billion times. A boredom that is really disrespectable," comments the devil. And in *Crime and Punishment* the satanic lecher Svidrigailoff makes the observation that, "Eternity always appears to us as an idea that man cannot grasp, as something monstrously huge. . . . But imagine that instead of that there will be a little room, like a bathhouse in the country, full of smoke, with spiders in all the corners, and that will be the whole of eternity." Yes, that will be hell, some eternally smoky corner in our world which has fallen out of relationship to God and has become totally meaningless. A "this-worldly eternal life," as it might be called, the monstrous self-contradiction of an eternal life *without* God, the unceasing historical-psychological course of all events *without* significance, in any case with only human, finite significance, without that great, critical, divine, other-worldly Whence and Whither that radically question all merely human signification. It would be the development of the earth and of humanity, together with their philosophies and religions, unendingly, *without* the absolute, other-worldly Why of God, which is at work in them, ever and again to be heard anew. It would be history *without* the divine crisis which makes an event qualified to be history. That is what hell is.

In such a world robbed of its meaning, even that event which first achieved for the world its other-worldly meaning—the sacrifice of Christ on the cross—has no more meaning. It has become an event alongside others. It is the one (perhaps the highest) of all the many possibilities in the wide field of historical-psychological reality, but therefore no longer what it is really intended to be: the end, the radical limitation, the crisis of this reality and its possibilities, and the announcing of the other, the true reality, God's reality. The devil knows how to pass by the cross without giving up his denial of God. "I was there," he relates, "when the Word of God, who died on the cross, entered heaven. I heard the rejoicing of the cherubim as they sang Hosanna, and the thunderous cries of delight of the seraphim that made heaven and the whole universe quake." But he cannot bring himself to shout Hosanna, for in such a Hosanna welling up out of hell, life would at once find its lost, eternal meaning, and in this meaning of the world that would reappear, the devil and hell would abolish themselves. "The necessary minus would immediately disappear . . . and with it, understandably, everything would be at an end," the devil says sarcastically. And as if in confirmation of this satanic wisdom, the starets Zossima gives voice to the divine insight, "Life is a paradise, and we are all in paradise, only *we do not wish to admit it.* But if we could recognize the fact, then tomorrow we would be in paradise."

That then is Ivan Karamazov's demonic conversation with himself. "There are some in hell," we read in the descriptions of the starets Zossima in the middle of the novel, "who have lived proud and cruel lives *in spite of their knowledge of the whole truth;* they are fearful and have given themselves over to the devil and his proud spirit totally and forever. For them hell is something voluntary and insatiable. They nourish themselves on their own malicious pride like a starving man in the wilderness, who sucks the blood out of his own body. They reject God's forgiveness and curse the God who calls them." In the works of Dostoevsky, this frightful, consciously suicidal contradiction of God is embodied in Ivan Karamazov. A few others who are demon-possessed may be placed at this side: deranged and suicidal men like Svidrigailoff in *Crime and Punishment* and Stavrogin and Kirilov in *The Possessed,* and erotics like Rogozhin in *The Idiot.* But they do not attain the excesses of Ivan. It is only a final consequence that out of the derangement of his spirit, out of the torment of his self-contradiction, out of such "a hell in his breast and in his thoughts" (as Alyosha once said), physical collapse should also result. To be sure, the doctor thinks it was the other way around. But what does a doctor know of the metaphysical bases of disease? What does he know of the fact that one can be sick with God, with unforgiven blasphemy, and die of it? Ivan perishes because of his demonic nature, and not because of his neurosis, and Dostoevsky has the devil laugh grimly over the doctors who want to cure him.

The shy, profound youth Alyosha is the only one who understands Ivan's illness. "The torments of a proud resolution, a deep conscience! The God, in whom Ivan did not believe, and the truth of God had overwhelmed his heart, which was unwilling to surrender." That is Alyosha's diagnosis. And does there not appear in this diagnosis a final, a last hope, the sole hope which there may still be for Ivan, who is sinking into the depths of hell?

> If I make my bed in hell, behold, thou art there.
>
> (Ps. 139:8b)

Can one be sick with God and die without there always being the supreme, the humanly impossible, the inconceivable possibility of being healed in God and of rising again? Not in vain did the starets impress the youth that he should pray for those out in the world who are dying in blindness: "Lord, have mercy on all who come before Thee." "Alyosha," we read, "smiled silently. 'God will be victorious!' he thought. 'Either Ivan will rise again in the light of truth or . . .' " (to be sure, this other satanic possibility of rejection remains; else how would grace still be *grace*?) " 'or he will perish in hatred,' added Alyosha bitterly and painfully, and then prayed once more for Ivan."

"And prayed once more for Ivan"—that remains the final word. Forgiveness can reach even into hell! At the end of his sinful speech to Christ, the devil-Grand Inquisitor waits, full of hatred, "for him to say something to him, even if it were something bitter, fearsome. But look, he silently approaches the old man and—kisses him softly on his bloodless, ninety-year-old lips. That is his whole answer."

This is the answer which Dostoevsky in *The Brothers Karamazov* wants to give to the monstrous godlessness of men. "God will be victorious." In this answer lies forgiveness, forgiveness also for the church which has betrayed Christ.

That is Ivan Karamazov, who, taken in his totality, signifies Dostoevsky's confrontation with religion and church and the revolt, hidden in them, of man against God. After severe struggles the height of pure knowledge of God finally appears. Only now is it clear that this world is *this world,* and the beyond is the *beyond,* that man is *man* and God is *God.* Only now are all Promethean lusts of man seen through and conquered. Now God is recognized as the one he is, and he has the honor which is his right.

Again and again there falls between the lofty evolutions of this gigantic movement of thought a glimpse into the depths of historical contexts. And it is not hard to perceive that Dostoevsky saw the church which had become idolatrous above all in the *Roman* church. It is just as clear that he found the embodiment of cultural atheism above all in the *west* European peoples. Ivan bears western traits even though he is inwardly Russian. Will we argue with Dostoevsky on this account? Will we want to escape the factual content and weight of the uncanny insights of Dostoevsky by reference to the Protestant church, or, as a wounded westerner, by a renewed complaint against "Russian attitudes"? We may do so if our consciences will allow us.

V | Knowledge of God

A final word remains to be said. It is that the power of this great critical dissolution and refounding of the world and of life in the knowledge of God was preserved in Dostoevsky in the acceptance of life, the understanding of man, the infinitely compassionate inclusion and movement of the whole fullness of those things that appear, in their need and hope, for which all his works are a single great witness. Where this world is recognized in its this-worldly quality and, precisely for the sake of this quality, is not rejected, because it is in its earthliness that there lies testimony to the eternity that encompasses all that is temporal and transitory, there this world can, yes, must be loved for the sake of that testimony in all its this-worldliness. Therefore the dying monk Zossima enjoins his disciples, "Love the earth and cover it with your kisses; love unquenchably, love everyone and everything, seek the inspiration of life. Moisten the earth with your tears of joy, and esteem this inspiration highly, for it is a great gift of God." Where the light of a final forgiveness shines now over all the crimes and sins of man, there even the most negative side of man, even abysses of vice, can no longer be treated as finally tragic, for the sake of the hidden positiveness of their witness to the grace of God. "Brethren, do not be repelled by the sin of man; love man even in his sin, for that is the image of the divine love." Herein lies the deep difference between

Dostoevsky and Leo Tolstoy, who throughout his whole life never progressed beyond this tragedy; the reason for this is probably to be found in the deep differences between their final presuppositions.

Where all that is human and positive is seen through in its total questionableness and relativity, where therefore no one can be conscious of a final advantage over another, where rather "everyone is in everything guilty before all" *(The Brothers Karamazov)*, there, precisely because of this common human questionableness, all mutual drawing of boundaries and cutting oneself off from others has lost all meaning. There all pharisaism, all desire to be in the right before others and to climb up over others has an end. There brotherhood is possible, yes, it is the sole command, beside which there is no longer any other. "Why are we fighting? Why are we trying to impress each other? Why do we not forgive each other?" *(The Brothers Karamazov)*. There the actual conditions are given for a new life of man together with man, given just in the judgment under which all are placed. There men find themselves again, find and recognize themselves in the great "solidarity of sin" *(The Brothers Karamazov)*, the only true solidarity there is on earth, in the deep need and perplexity of life, together enduring and awaiting their common salvation.

So in Dostoevsky there comes a full acceptance of life, of nature, and of man, a paradoxical affirmation of that which is, as it is, for the sake of that which it is *not*. The only proofs of this which can be adduced are his total work. But in certain passages this hot, compassionate love for all creation is given direct expression. The most powerful of these are the often quoted, well-known descriptions of the starets Zossima in *The Brothers Karamazov*. I will refrain from all further quotations. In order to quote well, one would have to quote everything. But one thing must be said in warning. One should not make too quick, too easy, too sure use of the wonderful words of this monk; under our hands, in our mouths, they can immediately lose their power (like the words of the Bible, and for the same reason!). For we easily overlook the fact that even here the Hosanna arises only out of the purgatorial fire of severest temptation, that thanksgiving comes out of a constricted breast, and that love for man and the world is drenched in tears. Not without reason do these glowing confessions of life swell from the mouth of one who is dying and will soon decay. Dostoevsky himself specifically made reference to the smell of decay in his saint, and he knew why: no deification of the creature is meant here with this love of life and of all creation; no religious heroics and sainthood are to be nourished here, not even under the cover of the finest love to God. The love of creature and of man which is proclaimed here is through and through an indirect and broken love. Out of "com-passion" in the literal sense is "the earth kissed," and the final meaning of this joy of life is the longing for a life totally different from what it is here and now, the longing for the transformation of all things, the longing for "paradise." "Each little leaf strives to speak, praises God, and cries to Christ, unbeknown to itself, and only through the secret of its sinless existence," says Zossima. The *sighing* of the creatures is the secret of nature, for the sake of which it can be loved. And the pathos of the inspiration of love which Zossima represents is sorrow; suffering—to suffer and bear suffering for everyone and for everything—is again and again proclaimed as the path of God's servants. This love is astonishingly negative and passive, different from all that we are otherwise accustomed to regard as love. Only in the great negations of I Corinthians 13 could it be adequately described: "Love envieth *not;* love vaunteth *not* itself, is *not* puffed up, doth *not* behave itself unseemly, seeketh *not* her own, is *not* easily provoked, thinketh *no* evil" (I Cor. 13:4b-5).

Therefore the pastoral work of the starets Zossima is astonishingly negative. It is not designed to remove men's burdens, to lead them out of the uncertainties of their lives, but
it is intended to lead men into them truly and for the first
time. For in bearing burdens, in persevering in the uncertainties of life, he sees (just as did the Idiot) the only way of redemption. "Except a corn of wheat fall into the ground and
die, it abideth alone: but if it die, it bringeth forth much
fruit" (John 12:24). This is the word written over the fate
of Mitya Karamazov, as it is also the motto of the whole book.
"Do *not* be content, woman, do *not* be comforted, accept *no*
comfort," he says to a mother who is inconsolable over the loss
of her son, in a wonderful scene at the beginning of the book,
when he counsels those who are seeking help. "Rather, weep,
but know in the hour when you weep that your son is one of
the angels of God, that he looks down on you from there,
rejoices in your tears, and shows them to God the Lord."
And to a sinful woman he speaks the remarkable words, "If
only regret is not impoverished in you, God will forgive you
all. Take care for regret, be untiring in regretting, but anxiety
you must drive away from you. Believe that God loves you so
much you cannot even imagine it, that he loves you *together*
with your sin and *in* your sin."

That is love for the creature and for man, the acceptance
of life as it is represented here. Stripped of its paradox, understood and taken directly and unbroken, this great admonition
to love would be turned into its opposite, it would become
eroticism, titanism, denial of God.

It is not only nature and man as such, but the dangerous
area of man's creations, culture, to which deep understanding
and active participation in creativity turn after all criticism
and with all criticism. Precisely there, where, in an *absolute*
critique of all that is human, Promethean lust is entirely
stifled, there and only there is the way free again for fruitful

and sober participation in culture. For it can never be the purpose of such criticism to curtail or endanger that which exists in its relative right by playing the absolute off against it in any given moment. If it did that, it would be chargeable with titanism, it would then fall into the temptation which Kant once described with the following words: "The light dove, as it cleaves the air in free flight and feels its resistance, could form the idea that it would succeed much better if there were no air." But not where there is no air, but rather only in the midst of the world as it is, only in the midst of and by means of the problematic facts of existence, does true knowledge arise and preserve itself.

Dostoevsky, again in distinction to Tolstoy with his often titanic criticism of society, knew this constantly and never forgot it. The absolute is God, and only God can play the role of God. He who knows that will become patient again, even in all pressing impatience and passion. He knows that it can never be for man a question of pursuing ultimate vanishing points, and therefore he will no longer play these final vanishing points off against that which exists, but he will seek in all that exists the secret relationships which refer to this ultimate. He will no longer issue a call to the building of a tower of Babel that reaches into the heavens; thus he has his hands free for joining in the work of building all the smaller towers of the earthly city, which is dear to him in its transitory nature, in its relativity and limitations, because it points to the entirely different heavenly city for which he is waiting. He no longer seeks to make the titanic stride of educating man into a superman, or even into a noble person; therefore he may and can rejoice in the many thousand modest steps that must still be made on earth in the present.

It is from this point of view that we may explain the remarkably indulgent, even positive position which Dostoevsky took in all his absolute criticism and basic sharpness toward everything that exists, especially the empirical state and the empirical church. I will not give individual examples here. The significant thing is the whole remarkably unimpassioned, factual, understanding, and forgiving manner in which he depicts thoroughly questionable political and social conditions. Often it seems to us he has *almost* too little anger and holy zeal to create something new. We might think of the total absence of social indignation even in his early work *Poor People*, which has poverty for its theme. We might think also of the court scenes at the end of *The Brothers Karamazov:* the total inner corruption of this justice, especially its corrupt psychology and handling of people is of course recognized and fully exposed, but he speaks of it without any moralistic pathos. How different it is in similar cases in the writings of Tolstoy. Compare, for instance, the bitterness and sharpness and poorly controlled passion of the judgment with which the latter almost without exception depicts his court scenes.

The classic example, however, of the unimpassioned, matter-of-fact way in which Dostoevsky sought for the hidden positiveness which can be contained in all, even the most unjust and horrible happenings, is his *The House of Death*, in which he depicted his Siberian prisons. He, if anyone, had the right to appear as the indignant accuser of the existing system. In his youth, by a miscarriage of justice, led out to the place of execution and then banished to Siberia, he returned after languishing for years—as the impassioned revolutionary perhaps? Full of hate because of the injustice he had suffered? No, as an obedient subject of his Czar, he writes his "memoirs" without any revolutionary pathos. But for that reason the other pathos in this remarkable book is all the stronger, the pathos of the deep understanding and forgiveness of even the most frightful human errors. And more than that, is there a stronger accusation anywhere than this book itself in which scarcely a single accusation can be found? Dostoevsky accuses directly and judges passionately only where he encounters the titanic gestures of man. These he finds most of all where man is not suffering and languishing, but is seeking justice in his own might and is building his towers of Babel. Thus the finger raised against socialism, thus the fist shaken against the culture of the West.

In the Siberian prisons he did not encounter these gestures. On the contrary, his strongest impression, the one overwhelming experience which he had there, was the meeting with humble, broken, suffering men. There he gained that insight into the hidden power of the knowledge of life and of the mastery of life, which is more alive in the poor and the impoverished classes of the people than it is among the clever and wise, the healthy and strong of this world. "Love" is what he calls this rare, hidden, paradoxical power, and he has the starets say of it, "Humble love is a fearsome power. It is the greatest power of all, and nothing can compare with it."

Dostoevsky never lost this respect for the humble people at the bottom of society, and he expected more from their hidden power than from all social and political reforms and revolutions. That is his faith in the people, that is his *conservatism*. Anyone who wants to get to know it in his own expression should read the remarkable letter from the year 1878 in which Dostoevsky turns to a group of enlightened, idealistically revolutionary students, and over against them takes into his protection the "raw people" with their uncorrupted sensitivity for truth and their faith in God.

It must be said that from this point also Dostoevsky took a conservative attitude toward the *church* of his people. He knew well the problematical nature of the church. He took his stand over against it in a position of radical critical insight, but here too he did not lose his perspective. Here too he preferred to wait amid the uncertainties rather than to attempt to break through into the vacuum of a churchless situation.

He knew that this attempt would never succeed, but would lead, like all other human anticipations of the kingdom of God, merely to a premature destruction of the eschatological tension that gives life its meaning. Here too he expected salvation, not from the overthrow of the church, out of which would immediately arise only a new church or a new sect, but again simply and solely from the radical power of those humble ones, who even in the church take the burden of the situation on themselves, whose prayer is genuine, because they stand like that publican in the depths of life, where nothing else remains for them except the strong, humble cry to God on high. Again it is the starets Zossima in whose mouth Dostoevsky places deeply meaningful words about the effect of these humble monks and believers, and in whom he presents to our eyes the figure of such a friend of God, who, through the midst of the dangerous and ambiguous region of religion and church, goes on his lonesome path, so open to temptation. Dostoevsky leaves no doubt that to stand in this struggle, to carry out these problematical issues, is particularly dangerous and fraught with temptations, but also has especially great promises and is especially needful. Those who fight this battle are the true church, in that without any pretensions, without even the pretensions of fighting the church or withdrawing from it, within the church they point beyond it and grow beyond it. Dostoevsky showed in the contradictions that blazed and crackled around the starets that they have to bear with particularly great enmity from the constituted defenders of the existing church, and that the latter would like nothing better than to see them driven out.

All that, however, should not be understood falsely in the sense of a justification of all that exists as it is. In it all there is no confirmation or glorification of the course of the world as it proceeds or of human ordinances as they are. Precisely this position, which seems so conservative, but in reality is so radical, is nothing else than one that raises the question of the problematical nature of life in its whole compass. It signifies the most powerful attack against all that exists, all that would preserve, make eternal, and deify itself as it is. *This* titanism is clearly recognized and fought against to the death. But is it necessary to repeat here what has already been said? The man Dostoevsky, taken as a whole, is one great, fiery protest against all that exists as such. It is not without cause that as often as we let Dostoevsky speak to us we feel the frightening anxiety over his growing influence, that we feel we are all somehow secretly attacked, threatened, constricted, and brought into question. For who is not dependent upon what exists? Who is not afraid of wandering into the wilderness, of the leap into the dark, the wager of faith toward which everything in Dostoevsky presses forward? And insofar as Dostoevsky revealed as no other, without fear of the consequences, the emptiness, the corruption, the readiness for judgment of all situations, he may well be called the "prophet of the Russian Revolution" (Merezhkovski). But inasmuch as the crisis in which he sees all that is human placed is incomparably deeper and more radical than Bolshevism ever dreamed, that would be saying too little.

Above all else this must be said: there where in Dostoevsky everything has as its goal and moves toward "resurrection," toward the final things, toward God's solutions, it cannot be other than that we shall find there already in the midst of time and this world wonderful parables and harbingers of this resurrection, which have an effect that is stronger, more transforming, more renewing than all the ever-so-titanic self-defense of man against the burden of existence. It is from this viewpoint that all those wonderful examples of the kingdom of heaven are to be understood, which in Dostoevsky's works again and again shine out of all the darkness and uncertainty of life like first, unbelievable rays that herald a new day for mankind. I am thinking, for example, of the starets Zossima's story of the officer who threw his pistol away in the woods before a duel. The deeper meaning of such traits can become clear for us if we think once again of the different way in which Tolstoy recounts similar scenes in his works. In Tolstoy[9] they appear almost without exception as the highest ultimate religious-moral accomplishments, with which man achieves entrance into a new life. In Dostoevsky, on the other hand, there is something which, though not without conflict, is not convulsive, something free, almost rejoicing in the worldly aspects of these "conversions," as they are called. They remind us of the conversions of publicans and sinners in the Gospels. But in Tolstoy the memory of *pietistic* struggles of penitence and conversion is unmistakable.

Moreover, in Dostoevsky's works, on the occasion of such breakthroughs and transformations there are none of those divisions into penitent and impenitent, righteous and unrighteous, children of God, and children of the world, which are inevitable in Tolstoy and the pietists of all ages, yes, which are precisely their goal and intention, while they never take place around the Jesus of the Gospels. On the contrary, there, world and God, the sinners and the righteous, come together. "He eateth with publicans and sinners." And Dostoevsky is somehow in the area of this occurrence when he tells how the "converted" officer finds after the duel for the first time a welcome among his still unconverted, worldly friends. "But now they all knew me and invited me to visit them daily. They laughed at me" (notice this total absence of any air of martyrdom!) "but they loved me." In Dostoevsky such occurrences never have the meaning that access for man

---

[9] In comparing Tolstoy with Dostoevsky I am not forgetting that Tolstoy at his best, in the stories of "The Master and the Servant," and "The Death of Ivan Ilitch" and others, is at times very close to Dostoevsky, but these little tales are not decisive for the main direction of his work.

to a new life can be forced. They are not the final, highest steps of religious-moral possibilities which man may yet be able to climb by exerting all his powers. They are rather first steps on the path of freedom which has already been entered on, and which becomes visible there where, in the depths of life, man has glimpsed the divine possibilities. They cannot be strained and forced, but they proceed rather out of the knowledge of God and of his eternal power, and serve only as its parables and illustrations. Therefore no special emphasis is placed on them. They nowhere spring out as purpose and intention. They are never deliberate. They are never demanded of man. They stand along the road like flowers. And to be sure, not by the road of especially holy men, or of those who strive and struggle, but by the path of declared children of the world, yes, of great sinners, of harlots and murderers, by the path of disreputable men, because it is not the path of the righteous, but the path of sinners that leads into the kingdom of forgiveness. And like flowers they fade again, these occurrences and experiences. There are no anticipations of the kingdom of God, no far-reaching religious movements, not even the presentation of visible and enduring personal sanctity and redemption. The saint decays, and his sanctity does not remain unassailed.

In Dostoevsky, the small and large gleams and examples of the divine light that breaks forth are triply guarded against the constantly threatening misunderstanding that this light finally is only, or perhaps once more, a merely *human* light. It remains at this: "God is *God*. He dwelleth in light unapproachable." Therefore even when one stands very near to him, yes, most especially there, it is possible to speak of his light only as of something absolutely paradoxical. Otherwise it is no longer *his* light that is spoken of. And yet it is precisely only of this light of *his* that Dostoevsky wanted to speak. All the traits and examples of new life are witnesses to the *divine*

possibility of forgiveness, which has been placed completely
beyond man's grasp. They are not to be confused with some
moral or religious soaring upward. Dostoevsky had no use for
that. He gives no examples for the collections of illustrations
for catechizing pastors. He has specifically and frightfully dis-
obliged the moralists. He never speaks of education as such.
The pedagogues (even the most modern and revolutionary)
must stand bewildered before him, unless they have an ear
for his word which opens the vista of a possibility that lies
beyond all attempts at education: "To *pray* is education."
The kingdom of God is not set up anywhere, but it is powerful in its coming, and harlots and sinners are the first to await
it. Understand that who can!

It is significant therefore that Dostoevsky never issued the
challenge which is almost the only one that Tolstoy ever issued: the challenge to become a *martyr*. On the contrary, this
possibility of finding a way out of the uncertainties of life was
included by Dostoevsky among those things which must be
unconditionally rejected. In "The Dream of a Ridiculous
Man," a late, deeply meaningful short story that says in a few
pages all that Dostoevsky had to say, it is told how men turn
away from God, from the true, living God, and thereby make
the earth into hell. And among the signs of this revolt is found
also this one: "Men learned to know sorrow and came to love
it. They yearned for torment and said that truth could be
bought only through *martyrdom*." In the pretentious attitude
of the martyr Dostoevsky saw *only* the titanic gesture of the
man who ultimately is seeking for himself even when he sacrifices himself.

For this reason he repeatedly issued another challenge, the
challenge to become like *children*. And again this was not
because he regarded and presented the child as such, in contradiction to all reality, as especially holy or angelic. But the
children in Dostoevsky's works have one advantage over the

adults; they still stand defenseless against life. They sense its uncertainties and its promises more deeply than do their teachers, and they still let themselves be oppressed or delighted by it without knowing the gamut of refined means, from indifference to hysteria, by which adults withdraw from the meaning of life. "Papa, what are they doing there?" calls the boy Raskolnikoff, when he has to watch a horse being tortured, and is beside himself with despair. "Come on, let us go," answers the father. But with a cry the boy breaks through the crowd, runs to the horse, throws his arms around the blood-spattered head of the dead animal and kisses it. Then he springs up full of rage, and with flailing fists throws himself against the driver. "Except ye repent and become like little children . . ."

In this full, passionate giving of one's self to whatever life brings with it every hour, in this absolute factuality and naïve defenselessness with which he confronts all impressions and answers them with anger, shame, or jubilation, in this lies the essence of the still uncorrupted child. To preserve for him this astonishment, fear, and delight is the only goal (again a *negative* goal!) of the education which, for example, the Idiot and Alyosha practice in their contacts with children. But it must be much more the goal of adults to return to the point where these children still stand. For in such men who have become children, who are resolute, gifted with a deep conscience, and inwardly motivated, there can awaken through a process of amazement and fear, slowly or all at once, that greatest thing that can awaken in man: *a consciousness of God.* Dostoevsky strove to awaken this consciousness, which is not to be confused with any moral or religious data, and which is already a part of "resurrection."

One final question remains. Was not Dostoevsky himself untrue to this knowledge? Did he not himself, in an extremely titanic manner, betray the eternal, the divine, the

Christ of the new life, the resurrection, the final things, by the here and now of a specific historical situation? We may think of his political position, of his own titanic passion, with which he believed in the future of Russia and fought for it, of the uncanny religious tones which he found for this political confession of faith. We think of the fact that for the sake of this goal he held that *all* means, including bloody wars of conquest, were permissible or even required.

There is no question about it; here everything must be conceded. We are standing at the point where Dostoevsky's own life appears in a highly questionable light. To excuse him here would be to misunderstand him. Yet we must seek one final time to get to the bottom of the matter. Dostoevsky's thinking has two poles: life as it is, the world as it goes its way, is one, and the beyond, "resurrection," eternity, is the other. Here is man, there God. Dostoevsky's total knowledge consists in the strict critical relationship of these two moments to one another, as he portrayed it. But what he does *not* know— or knows only all too well in its demonic danger!—is that in-between world where man becomes God and the other-world becomes this-worldly, where the dream is dreamed of being like God, of the development of man from "gorilla to superman." It is just this idolatrous dream which Dostoevsky saw was being dreamed in the West above all, in the form which is so well known to us, of cultural evolution toward leagues of nations, yes, to the union of all mankind and finally to the automatic arrival of the kingdom of God and universal peace. Now there formed in Dostoevsky's mind the plan—equally Promethean—of creating in *Russia* a bulwark against this western poison. Now it was a matter of that gigantic conception of the holy Russian people. Now Dostoevsky himself dreamed that dream of power in which there finds embodiment that which can never find embodiment anywhere as such, not even in the Russian people. For there are no *holy* peoples, and there is no *Russian* Christ. This should be noted by the admirers of Russia among us! Else what particular task would there be in Russia for the Christ of "The Grand Inquisitor"?

Perhaps, however, even this grotesque aberration of Dostoevsky's is still better than the dream of the West, for its deepest root—even though distorted to titanism—is the counterattack against that western idea of the rise of mankind *without* God. Again and again at the culmination of these political conceptions of Dostoevsky's there breaks forth the totally supra-political proclamation of his deep perception of God, the spreading abroad of which he held to be Russia's holy mission.

Still, we do not want to whitewash Dostoevsky. These monstrous outgrowths of his thought belong to his portrait. We do, however, want to grant him that understanding of the titanic element in man, which he possessed and displayed to such a high degree. At this point he himself is one of those problematic figures out of his works. He is *not* a saint, *not* an ascetic; he is not a noble soul but a demonic one. He is *not* Tolstoy; he is Dostoevsky, and he has an earthly name and an earthly countenance. He stands before us as a *man*. He too is what he is for us only in refraction through his humanity, only indirectly. Even he himself, on the basis of the paradoxical knowledge of man's situation between heaven and earth, is to be justified only from the viewpoint of *God*. He himself stands deep within the uncertainties of his work, not somewhere above them or beside them. But it is precisely this which gives his life, his fate, his human portrait, the greatness which is his. His face bears the traits of his work and his work the traits of his face. Religion, cult, saint worship, are *not*—in spite of Merezhkovski!—to be made out of him. He is the witness, not the messiah. He is a likeness, not the thing itself. Just for that reason he *is* witness and will be heard, he *is* full of allusion, full of likenesses, full of meaning! For that reason there is revealed in the traits of his work, though they are transient and expendable like all that is earthly, that *imperishable* trait of *eternal* reality for which he searched so passionately all his life.

Made in the USA
Las Vegas, NV
05 August 2021

27653485R00049